THE LYRICIST FIRM

ONE FAMILY...
ONE LOVE!!!

THE FIRM DIVAS

PRESENTS

VOLUME II

https://www.facebook.com/thelyricistfirm
https://www.facebook.com/firm.divas
https://twitter.com/#!/thelyricistfirm
http://www.thelyricistfirm.com

HIT US UP!!!

FIRM:
Not soft or yielding when pressed; comparatively solid, hard, stiff, or rigid: not shaking or trembling; steady: a firm voice. Not likely to change; fixed; settled; unalterable: a firm belief. Steadfast or unwavering, as persons or principles: indicating firmness or determination: a firm expression.

DIVA:
1. To describe a person who exudes great style and personality with confidence and expresses their own style and not letting others influence who they are or want to be.
2. A person whose character makes them stand out from the rest.
3. Noun; a person's title in a group of friends or in a society that is popular or famous and who many people try to copy.
4. A person who tries to achieve what they want and who does not let people get in their way, and doing so with style and class.

SISTERHOOD:
The state, or kinship of being sisters.
The quality of being sisterly; sisterly companionship.

We are the ladies of The Lyricist Firm. We are Mothers, Lovers, Survivors, Writers, Poets and Storytellers. We are Creators of art, with our love for poetry we share our voice. Through our writing we bring our hearts, our lows and our triumphs.
We bring a unique bond, women from all over the country different ages, different walks of life we all come with a great love and respect for one another we come together
As sisters, we come together as The Firm Divas....

THE FIRM DIVAS

TABLE OF CONTENTS

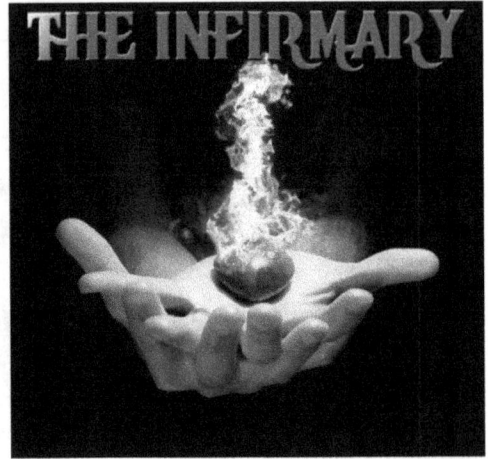

THE FIRM DIVAS

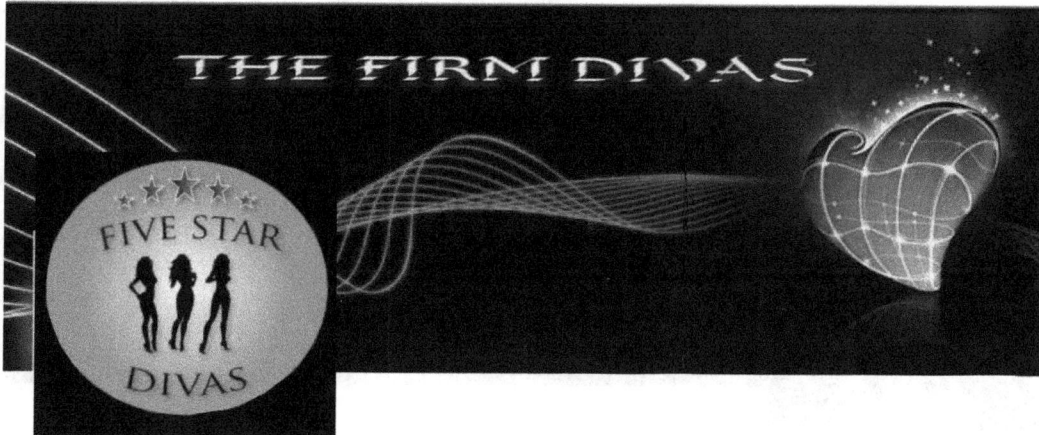

THE FIRM DIVAS

THE FIRM DIVAS

The Firm Prophets
United in Christ

UNITED IN CHRIST

FIRM:
Not soft or yielding when pressed; comparatively solid, hard, stiff, or rigid: not shaking or trembling; steady: A partnership or association for carrying on a business. The name or title under which associated parties transact business: The Lyricist Firm

PROPHETS:
A person who speaks for God or a deity, or by divine inspiration. A person who practices divination. A person who foretells or predicts what is to come: a weather prophet; prophets of doom. A spokesperson of some doctrine, cause, or movement. The Firm Prophets exists to help you grow spiritually with other Christians. Follow Christian writers and topics; learn the Bible with daily devotionals, Bible study and more to help you grow in your Christian faith.

Jesus taught us to let our light shine and be salt in this world (Matthew 5). How can we reach others with the Good News of Jesus Christ? This Topic Hub discusses how to share your faith with others, church outreach, and how to communicate God's love to a world in need.

Establishing daily devotionals is a key to growing closer to God and experiencing more victory and peace in your life! Take a few minutes each day to be alone with God and prayerfully read from "The Daily Bread"

www.christianbackgrounds.net

A Diva Message

FROM PWP

* * * OFTEN IMITATED * * *
* * * BUT NEVER * * *
* * * DUPLICATED * * *

RIDDLE ME THIS ???

WHY is THE FIRM so DAMN HATED ???

Cause we fuck'n originated / leave'n fake lames frustrated / but fuck it... steal the name / A Family under siege / fuck it... steal the fame
You will feel the flame / so know this to be true / the definition of a fact / is the hoe-bitch in you
I'll shoot a flow through you... STOP IT... FOXXX drop it...
BY: POETICAL WORD PLAY

*The **SISTERHOOD*** can't be duplicated... ***THE DIVAS*** bring so much to the table... UNITED WE STAND TALL... NO hater will makes us fall... Women with such class... Men want us and we don't have to show ass... Our wordz speak for them self... ***TLF Girlz*** we will defend... when an attack comes on... it'z your pride on the mend... started as a dream... We have ***FIRM**ly* become reality... We grace this space... with a Sisterly bond... with one thing in common the love of wordz... so trying to bring us down is unheard... till the end of time our wordz will live... sometimes people need to see that they can burn that bridge... attack us at will... do it for the frill... but at the end of the day... ***THE DIVAS ARE HERE TO STAY***...
BY: MS.F0XXXY

THE FIRM DIVAS

No need for that / put that back on the whack on the shelf / cause a bitch is a trick that / killed their self

You wanna open up a can of make believe / and spread your fungus all about like a skin disease

And test these degrees like a food inspector / but here comes Brooklyn / the fool rejecter

With that "GET A LIFE" injector / feed'n your brain / waterproof reflector / cause I can't stand the rain

I can't stand a damn lame / where they do that shit at / if you're worried about your name / I threw that shit back

You can keep it in-fact / and you know who you are / you want fame fuck around / and I will make you a star

Angelically far / DAMN... the host with the most / trip'n on this Firm'post / talk'n to a ghost

You don't really wanna roast / with a team you can't handle / I will light you like a candle / I already can't stand you

Sick tricks is off the handle / but you can't (Hammer) "Touch This" / Divas stand up / and show these clowns who's the roughest!!!

I aim and bust that / puss out your fuck'n neck / call you collect / and pitch you some disrespect like

Fuck your internet wreck / this is CHAMPIONS money / you better off fuck'n off / not attack'n us dummy

You couldn't take nothin from me / but a smack in the face / sick trick I will flip / and kick the hole in your space

You fuck'n loco disgrace / want'n to bang with my Ladies / these are The Firm Divas / to you fuck'n fugazies

Imitation Shadies / WTF / will the real Eminem please / STAND THE FUCK UP

That's what I thought / so what's up you lame ass / I see your ass snake'n / so I'm cut'n the grass

Revoke'n your pass / and flunk your ass-out for effort / with an F for lack of method / and not check'n my record

I can't be disrespected / when I... hush up you liars / and I'm very undetected / when I spark like brush fires

THE FIRM DIVAS

I flush what don't inspire us / you writers ain't desirous / say what you will to the lame / but don't kick it and lie to us

You never been fly to us / we just patted your back like... / good little flunky / cause that's where you was at right

But now it's a wrap / and you're on the wish list / you can't come back you little brat / so... go marry Christmas!!!

We know y'all miss this / lyrical clique / full of lyrical clit / you miss this lyrical dick

Lyrical tricks / don't you know that's for kids / I know you're a little mental / due to technical SIDS

You'll get your face lifted kids / when you off the grown / Masters of the throne / with a disastrous tone

We can get it on clowns / I got a Microphone too / and I don't need a crew / to dismantle the likes of you

You can build your crew / and you can boss 'em all / but give 'em a Biggie Warning / cause I will toss 'em all

I'll bounce you little bitches / like a I was play'n basketball / tell them bastards all / line up for casting call

I'm Brooklyn out lasting all / like your favorite legend / the same sea you drown in / is the water I'm tread'n

So now your ass is dead in / my neck of the woods / cause niggas round here / don't buy make believe goods!!!

It's a FIRM/DIVA shit slaughter / get these clowns some shit water / put it in their mouth / then choke them fools out

They wanna throw names out / we'll blow their brains out / that'll put the flames out / and dump their lame out

Let their fake friends shout / and come to their rescue / birds of a feather / flock together like the rest do

Like HYPNOTIQ said: God Bless 'em / call their next of kin / see the flood gates are open / somebody let them clowns in

Now they PeterPan pretend ± like this shit don't faze them ± thinking they're electrified ± like a Five'0 tazer

But fuck their life major ± and I'm done with these games ± now let's get back to THE FIRM and FIRM DIVAS fuck lames!!!

BY: POETICAL WORD PLAY

A DOZEN OF ROSES

He gave me a dozen of roses,
which made my eyes sparkle.

He gave me a dozen of roses,
to win me over and he did.
I thought that was out of his heart,
but it was only to charm me into his dangerous trap.

He gave me a dozen of roses,
I was greener in the nose than I am now
didn't realise he was playing my own mind against me.
Many red flag warnings were given me,
but I was busy trying to find true love
when really it was about those 12 roses
doing all the work not you damn lol.
You had me for a while.

He gave me a dozen of roses,
should of regonized back then,
when I didn't say thank you right away to your liking,
you bitched up,
and threw a hissy fit because of that,
it had me puzzled in the face and lil' I must admit,
I felt for the moment like real shit.
The only thing that's not a mess
and which was a blessing is my son.
If I didn't get anything else good,
it was my son DAMIUS.
And that's worth way more that some fuckin roses,
matter of fact, he's PRICELESS.
He gave me a dozen of roses!!!

BY: LAVENDER LADY

A SUNRISE IS THE SUNSET IN COLORADO

I woke up this morning to greet the sun!
To have it warm me some!
And I thought of all my loved ones here under this sky!
But I couldn't help but be a lil down!
Cause I miss the cali sunset bright and lively" Colorado sunsets took my
breath away.
And the sunrises.
Damn that what I mean they are so beautiful
And an they play with your soul brighten you closer
Light refraction off of snow and ice on to the land around.
Colorado sunrise sunset!
a Cali sunrie sunset a washigton sunrise sunset.
A sunrise in That land of the sun!!! Those I long to see!!!
BY: NEEDAQUEEN

Promises of the most amazing sunset,
visions I'll neva forget,
I long to wake to the sunrise,
better yet to watch it in ur eyez,
to be in your arms under the most clear and romantic night skies,
like you can reach out and grab a star,
the best place by far,
the freshest greenery,
beautiful scenery,
gonna love it for many reasons,
gorgeous thruout the seasons,
from sunny days to snow covered land,
it's the home of my man,
my future home, the place where my heart was found,
I'm Colorado bound!!!
BY: L4DY B

THE FIRM DIVAS

The clouds eliminate a picture of one I see every day,
The sunrise brightness to my eyes,
A new day a new dawn,
Colorado brings the beauty out of things,
Like the birth of a baby fawn,
To the essence of the river flow,
To the light over the mountains of a sunset s glow,
I dream of a day when it might be a you and me,
A day when I will drink up the sunrays you radiate,
Where my heart will be free,
Where we will meet and see our destiny!!!
BY: MS.F0XXXY

ALONE JOURNEY

The projector is flashing before my eyes.
The many encountered hello's and good-byes.
Some with many charms,
some with the intent to do harm.
Some with a heart to go the extra mile, Some not wanting to stay awhile.
Out of all the choices that were made, Why did I choose the one I did?
May never understand why,
but thank God for two beautiful kids.
New journeys to travel, putting feet to gravel, walking in territory unknown.
The terrains of changing times, forsaken past left behind... direction
appearing blown.
Solitude is an antagonist that does not exemplify the character of me.
In the arms of a leading co-star is where my heart desires to be.
Dramatically inclined,
without ever trying out for this solo monologue.
Can I please modify the story to include a second person part?
Rehearsed lines, words intertwined,
starring my " Love".... to capture my heart.
Journey ahead... sore and worn feet... persistence no defeat!!!

BY: CARAMELCAKE54

Anthem Of Poetry

Streaks of color across the sky, losing focus without worrying why, its not the only loss of the day, always thought it would end this way... friends and poets gather round, time to put this sorrow in the ground, dance and sing round the fire, voices, spirits rising higher, food and drink do freely flow, as purple hued melody plays in nature's symphony, crescent moon watches lazily, slips of paper filled with regrets fed to the beast, start tomorrow with a clean slate, give through sweat your sacrifice... no crimson tears required tonight, feel the steele drum throb within, experience heartbreak with the violin, here comes the flutes and clarinets, magical fairies fill the air, sparkling dust everywhere, the sax brings thoughts soft and low, slowing our sway as tensions grow, stand within the flames with me... I see God....what do you see?... freely give n freely take the offering to celebrate... throw off the shaw of conformity... stand up, be heard, sing with me... the wordless anthem of poetry!!!

BY: MAJESTICLADY

As The Tears Flow

As I sit here and remember when

The tears of joy are followed by regret
I am sure if I allow the tears to flow
that someday I will know...

Was my fears just to great,
and my Faith too little too late...

Do I deserve a second chance?
As the tears flow I ask where was I
when yours flowed from your eyes?

Is life so cruel it does not allow for mistakes n wrong choices?

Am I destined to walk this earth alone?
Have I just caused to much hurt?

This is just a few of the reasons my tears flow...
Untold riches of my heart and Soul just not being seen
and this is the consequence of my own making....

As the tears flow my Soul slowly heals
how much water does it take to be wash free of sins and mistakes?

As my tears flow I wish only for whatever is best nothing less!!!

BY: TONICE

ASHES TO ASHES, DUST TO TRUST

Waking up this morning,
to the flip side of the coin,
asking myself already today,
how do I keep on goin,
the sun shining through,
what is coming my way,
do I adjust my point of view.

If love is meant for knowing,
how can I trust a stranger,
cause the love my past was showing,
kept my heart in danger.

Welcome to the other side,
I once held joy but now its pain,
struggling to keep up with the tide,
but I'm swimming against in vain.

So many broken pieces,
my heart a mosaic of glass,
which piece will you choose,
to never give me back?

I have sent many more,
in the essence of my tears,
pain melting them down for you,
liquefied through my fears.

THE FIRM DIVAS

I have felt true treachery,
so I know nothing but beguiled,
this is just another day,
a heart with so little left,
creates its own debauchery,
and lives on the outskirts of love,
so wild,
so free.....

So to my window,
let the sun shine,
but I will not trust the glow,
for it was never mine!!!

BY: ARTICHOKEHEART

*A*WAKEN *R*AIN

Awaken by the sounds of the gnawing rain.
Deep slumber providing renewal and strength to gain.
Delightful dreams that dance to a melodic tune.
Escalating desires that go thump and boom.
Thunders that roar with all their might.
The lonely wishing they were in someone's arms tonight.
The sound of the rain on the windowsill.
Provokes thoughts yearning to be revealed.
Drops of rain in the form of tears.
Cleansing sight, erasing fears!!!

BY: CARAMELCAKE54

BATTLEFIELD

They said love is a battlefield
If you ever been in love you'll know this is real
Sometimes a hug and a kiss will seal the deal
That may or may not last a life time
When you didn't run at the first sign
Because we all knows that love comes and it goes
Some people don't know how to let things go
Some don't know how to let their feelings show
But its one thing that you're never know
If you don't open your heart up and let someone in
Let them learn you from the outside in
Why do some people start things off that way
I wish I knew
That's why some relationship just don't stay
But the ones that does
Know the true meaning of love
They been on that battlefield
They have a bond that was seal
And a love that is real
Always a true fight will make things right
So they can lay up close together in their loves arms each night
They know the true meaning of being on that battlefield
That it would makes things better and their life
would move more smoothly and end up being just right.
But if don't
That's part of the battle
and the worst thing is to be left standing
Out there on that battlefield alone!!!

BY: ATLANTAMOODY

BE NOT...

Be not decieved by what you see,

there's a ready beast within,

be not convinced by what you hear...

only what you alone feel...

be not led nor left by my steps...

lead me or take my hand...

be not impatient...

take the time...

rewards divine...

be not misunderstood in your quest to understand...

truth through heart...

believing spirit...

competent hands...

deliver wisdom to the land!!!

BY: MAJESTICLADY

BETTER OFF ALONE

Now I can honestly say you never beat me,
But it hurts just as bad the way you mistreat me,
respect my personal space,
and get the fuck out my face,
For I catch me a case,
You walkin thin ice and that's a dangerous place,
To real men you a fukkin disgrace,
This usually a back and forth game,
But today it ain't the same,
Ain't no running back, I'm over you,
Me leavin was so overdue,
You ain't nothin but and ex,
Good for nothin but the sex,
Kept you around cause I loved ya stupid ass, but I don't need you,
Nigguh I'm the one feed you,
I don't depend on you for shit,
You're a bad habit, I need to quit!!
that's more clear after every hit,
you're a bitch and a half,
The typa nigguh make a bitch laugh,
Being ya level of clown should be a fukkin crime,
Can't take you serious half the fukkin time,
nigguh you a joke,
Weaker than that shit you smoke,
Fuk you and every word you spoke,
ya you hurt me, but I ain't broke,
I'm too strong a woman to crumble at the hands of a man,
took my heart n ran,
New vision, new plan,
I might stand alone,
But a bitch better off alone!!!

BY: L4DY B

BOUND

Bound to these chainz,
my mind must refrain,
from these lucid thoughts,
seaping through my brain,
yes I'm just a dame,
with nothing left but my name,
I'm bound by the hurt of a thousand years,
the darkness hides my tearz,
lost in a dwindling sea,
my body just wantz to flee,
like that pesky rodent,
it burrows deep within me,
a multitude of Angelz surround me,
and say sister,
this cannot be,
you are bound by only what the devil wantz you to see,
a trumpet playz in the distance,
I hear but can I listen,
I see what was becoming of me,
my tearz began to fall,
drip drop,
flip flop,
I beg God for mercy,
I beg Him to release me,
to please set me free,
this bondage is costing my life.
I need to see You are my Light,
need to see without you,
I'll never rise through the ashes,
and I'll continue to be bound by these lashes,
my freedom starts with peace!!!

BY: MS.F0XXXY

BURNING BRIDGES

As I look across the bay,

I see it's another sad day,

today I've burned those bridges away,

tried to do right and not cause any strife,

but the time has come to let go,

time to run away, get away from the pain,

by going through it I have nothing to gain,

past mistakes have come unglued,

sometimes it seems rude,

the sea rages wild, like a unruly step child,

waves come crashing down,

so sad with no one around,

the ashes smolder until the dawns early light,

my future has never seemed less bright,

the winds of change are calling all the same,

now it's time to burn that bridge that calls your name!!!

BY: MS.F0XXXY

CAREFREE LOVE

Smell the aroma of flowers blowing in the wind.

Pleasant fragrance permeating from deep within.

Meticulous meadows untouched but kept clean.

Hearts happy with joy, smiles shine with gleam.

Relaxing and relishing in the presence of our dream.

Appreciating the simple things in life,such as ice cream.

All doubts and fears all pushed aside.

Humble beginnings not filled with pride.

No hidden agendas, no secret pretenders, just open and care free.

An old fashioned romance that's meant to be!!!

BY: CARAMELCAKE54

CHAINS

I'm pulling my chains.
Dragging them across the floor.
Banging on the door, Let me out!
Nobody hear my shout.
So I'll just sit back in my corner and wait...

Maybe the day will come,
when your hate for me is over.
Releasing me from the chains that bind me...

Bound to a life I did not chose.
In the end,
you know you'll lose...

Holding me captive,
against my will,
is a good way to kill,
my love for you...
I've picked at the lock many times over the years,
just to find my tears,
rusted it...

Trusted as a friend,
you became my lover.
Obsessed with me,
that's over...

Sick in your mind,
the demons,
plague you.

THE FIRM DIVAS

Pulling at the bars of my cell,
trying any way to get free...

Can't you see?

Are you blind?
I'm here, but I'm not.
Once these chains are off,
I'm gone...

Silence is yours,
sing a sad song of how I did you wrong.
No audience?
I'll clap for you,
my final goodbye...

Heres your chains,
the dungeon is open.
Take the steps,
easy does it.

Click! Goes the lock.
Now you're the one who's a prisoner,
have fun.
I'm done...
Free at last!!!

BY: DARKANGEL68

CHISELED IN MY MEMORY

Chiseled in my memory bank

This heavenly creature....

Yo stunning angelic silhouette

In my mind a

Total prisoner for life

Deep deep long stirs

Who you be baby girl?

Instant chemistry given birth

My innocent looks keep getting stuck on you

Heart beat stop and pause

As we stand face to face

Not sure about what all of this mean

Finally

We both return to earth

Not sure of just what happened

Heavens it sure felt good

In passing ...

excitement is always

Released

As my mind goes airborne

One more time

On another fantasy

Where total bliss is given birth!!!

BY: PURE ECHO PLAY

Creating memories from a distance allows the imagination to flow

Thoughts of you in stallion attire and saxophone to blow

Playing the melodrama of our separate lives.

Escalating into realms of sharp notes that climb and then dives.

Harmoniously happy with gleeful sparks of joy

Appreciating a full grown man, that's no longer a boy

To dance the song of love and too behold the rarest of gems

Peculiar qualities that make you stand out from the rest of them

Fantastic fantasies orchestrated from the heart

Chiseled in my memory... is how we got off to a good start!!!

BY: CARAMELCAKE54

Church Bitches

It's sometimes hard to spot a church bitch a mile away.

They may dress modest and be one that mainly prays.

The ones that you can clearly see what their game is, strolling down the aisle with high heels.

Their shirt is Refusing to hold their breast.

Causing men who are strong much distress.

The skirt is way above the knees; they wanna distract and be the biggest unspoken tease.

They say a man comes to church to lead a woman astray.

Same can be said for a church bitch.

Having ladies wondering why she showed up that day.

Having men lusting after them, when they are trying to focus on the Lord.

Wrecking homes and causing discord.

They pretend to be your friend and lend a hand.

Just to get closer to your preacher man.

They laugh and smile in your face, all along dreaming they were in your place.

They want you to trust them and confide, even offering the pastor a ride.

She can't wait to get him alone, so she can be the biggest snitch, him not realizing that she's just a church bitch.

When they supposed to be believing God for their own man.

THE FIRM DIVAS

Along desiring to take your husband.

A church bitch can be one of the most dedicated chicks in church.

Pretending to be on a deep spiritual search.

They sit and say hallelujah, praise the Lord and amen.

They may even fall on the floor, til another fine man walks thru the door.

Then when she steps back in her flesh, and do it in a twitch.

She resumes her role as a church bitch!!!

BY: CARAMELCAKE54

CONFUSED

When the sun goes down at night
I know I ended my day with another fight
I have feelings for you but it just ain't right
Should I be happy or should I be sad
But whichever one it is
I always have the comfort of my Mom and Dad
They will hold me up and push me forward
But could any men be straightforward
Still at night my loneliness fills up my room
No one to turn too
am I doom
Crying quietly on the inside
Those flowing tears I'm trying to hide
My feeling is taking my body on a ride
But you know what I can't get mad
All I know is that every time I try to get close to someone it just don't last
How could you talk to someone for hours
And act like you're in love and feeling someone like you're under their
powers
I wish I could understand the ways of the human mind
So I wouldn't be wasting my time
Getting to know someone that only cares about their selves
And will not even look back when they hurt someone else
You know the one and other person who cares
I run into this so much those days
It has me confuse should I stay or should I run away
This isn't easy for me to open up like I do
Sharing to all the would my feelings I have for you
If you're reading this I would never know
Forever open would be my door.
To my heart and mind which is filled with doubts
But getting to know you
You have found a direct route
Into my heart but don't worry I want push myself on you
You know where I'm at and just what to do!!!

BY: ATLANTAMOODY

DADDY MAY I

Daddy, can I go out to play?
Cause daddie I wanna have some fun today?
Daddie, I'm tired of being in the house.
I want a new book daddy, Ise tired of reading about a mouse.
Daddy, can you take me to the library?
I wanna be smart like you..
Daddy, can we stop at the dollar store to buy some super glue.
I promise not to put it on my head.
I promise Daddy you won't have to send me to bed.
Daddy, may I have new sandals, and a new dress?
I promise Daddy I won't make a mess.
Daddy, can we go to Mickey D'S?
I like that food daddy, it taste better than yours...oops sorry daddy I didn't
mean to say that. Daddie I take that back.
Daddy, can I have over my friend named Mike?
I promise not to let him ride with me at the same time on my bike.
Daddy, why men have a stick?
Daddy, the neighbor made me lick.
Daddy, he told me I was pretty and he gave me some change.
Daddy are you ok? Why are you looking strange?
Daddy, where are you going and why you grabbing your gun?
Dadd,y may I go have some fun?
You know I'm your little girl, and Daddy you're the best Daddy in the
world!!!

BY: CARAMELCAKE54

DIVA LOVE

Not only a lady at all times…
I am a woman with a strong mind.

Refined…

Soft spoken, short & sweet.
Yet my msg. carries power.

Deep…

Not 1 to play with,

Diva Amor will take down a bitch.

So take note & don't forget.

To my sisters... Much luv & respect

BY: TRANQUIL AMOR

Hey my Sistas this is Diva_Prettyeyez.
I'm real cool, but do keep it real.
I love writing my poetry,
and I write down whatever I feel,
or what's on my mind.

It's a real honor that you excepted me in as A Diva.

Thank you,
and much respect...

BY: LAVENDER LADY

DIVA ROLL CALL
(FEAT. ECHO)

Diva Roll Call
Assume
The military stump
Mind at attention
Hut! Hut!
In rhythm
Let's get cracking
Cock up
yo ink pens
Give yo fingers a stretch
Pep up
Yo vibrato
Tisk, Tisk… Dispatch those words
Let's show them
we really mean business
Unleash that gangsta shuffle step
United
Is what
We all about
Good will so vigilant
Ain't even afraid to ruffle a few feathers
In the name of our DIVA Thang!!!
BY: PURE ECHO PLAY

An anthology, of literary artistry...
Splash colorful words, across a blank canvass... A masterpiece creation, from gifted hands... That move to the feel of emotion... Producing a vivid notion... Brought to life, in third dimensional motion... Pulling minds into telepathic sensory... Delving deep into the psyche, of an artiste. A stimulating journey, of imagery and reality... Fantasy and actualities. Provocating is she... With the ability, of words... To move and stir, stagnancy... To revive circulation, to the deadened, and pump life through the veins once again. She, is each Diva... Special, each and every one... It is the contrast and comparison, that

THE FIRM DIVAS

is the balance... Their strength... They are resilient! It's their time, to shine...
To spread their wings, and fly...
Diva's, rise!!!
BY: TRANQUIL AMOR

Poetry in my heart,
Emotion in my art,
A true diva from the start,
These words that I write,
Is what got me thru the fight,
In my world of darkness they shed a lil bit of light,
My last bit of hope,
thru these words is how I cope,
My own personal brand of dope,
Give me strength when im in need,
A poem made from everytime I bleed,
Encouragement for me to succeed,
I *am... L4DY B*!!

They said we looking for self-reflection
But they don't wanna come in our direction
Pen and paper in hand
We're more united then an marching band
Words bleed from our pens
Like blood leaks from your viens
When the Divas words hit you
Believe me you're never be the same
Standing proud and tall
Divas from the heart we will never fall
They tried to take us down once before
But the underestimated that sister love
And with pride we show their ass the door
We are one and all and the Divas would never fall
We stepping up to another scale
So be ready the Divas would never fell
BY: ATLANTAMOODY

Ta la da

THE FIRM DIVAS

Fly Fly Fly
Here is Diva xx.tonice.xx
Saying Hello
Hope all is well for you
I am here to say I have a new
prospective to be sharing in my poems
War in the streets
war in the head
Survivors will be all along
Here today is a gift
Food, housing and warmth
Friendly faces or enemies watching
Paranoid or cautious
Balance or extreme
Eye of the beholder
Behold your life
next step in life is to LIVE!!!
BY: TONICE

DIVAS;
Looking for self-reflection,
Each interpretation is perfection,
The screen our easel,
Our fingers our ink,
Lovers of beautiful words,
Nouns and verbz,
A fine wine,
Aged and timeless,
Itz Diva time
our star shinez with such brightness,
Words, Unaltered,
Dateless, Unchanged,
A sisterly love,
Exchanged,
We are here to stay!!!
BY: MS.F0XXXY

DOES HE KNOW

Does He Know that I cry at night.

Does He Know that I am broke down and feel left out.

Does He Know that I want a baby but from what the doctors say it like they saying it is hopeless.

Does He Know my pain is way too deep for one person to try and solve.

Does He Know the pain, stress, and the loneliness takes a strong hold on my body and it wears and tears constantly at my soul.

Does He know that I need him to send an angel to my side because I do get very scared and I need a hand near me at all times.

Does He Know that I am getting weary and I need someone strong and someone that's never going to leave my side but stay forever.

DOES HE KNOW IS WHAT I WANT TO KNOW!!!

BY: MAIYEN THE CHRISTIAN

DON'T MISTAKE RED FLAGS FOR RED ROSES

Don't mistake red flags for red roses. No matter how charming he may be or how he poses. He may claim to have just moved to town. When actually every block he has been around. He may be attentive unlike any other. May claim to be the only one left in his family without a sister or brother. The words he say may flow sweet in your ear. To ease your mind of any apprehension and fear. He may have an accent that you never heard in real life. He says you will be his wife. He starts to ask you to do things you would not normally do. He claims to love and only wanna be with u. Online bank account in your name, claiming to be new to US, needing somewhere to let his money rest. He shut you out of your own account u started for him. Your knight in shining armor is starting to look dim. He promises to shower you with trips and the world. When he has no intentions of making you his girl. You start to feel like shit when you realize he's a counterfeit. When your world starts to crumble down. Your Prince Charming is nowhere to be found!!!

BY: CARAMELCAKE54

DREAMING OF A PLACE

I'm dreaming of a place
where I can just be me

A place
where I'm free to love and
live life like I am meant to be

A place
where I can smile
or cry for no reason

A place
where my feeling can
change just like the seasons

A place
where I can be around people
that can bring joy to my life

A place
where they're kids playing
and no times for fights

A place
where the sun shines bright

A place
where I can just enjoy the sights

A place
where I can lay in my lover arms
and make love all night

A place
where I can listen to
my favorite music as it plays

A place
where I can relax
and soak in the rays

A place
where I would forever
plan to stay

A place
where I can dream
about it every day!!!

BY: ATLANTAMOODY

ENDLESS LOVE

Softly I feel your touch,
Baby,
I need you so much,
whisper,
sweet melodies,
of that endless love,

Time will stand still,
till Im near you again,
If only in my dreamz,
I cherish,
our memories,
Making love,
in the sand,
walking hand and hand,

Two souls become one,
if only for a moment,
in time,
Excited,
to see me,
wanting you to touch my body,
make love to me till I can't breathe,

Sing a song,
of love,
forever you will be in my heart,
wish that our souls would have never part,

I will love you,
for all of my days and nights,
for you are my endless love!!!

BY: MS.F0XXXY

ETERNAL FLAME

Rivers flowing suddenly dry..
eyes opened once blind...
questions echo with answers denied...
what will it be...
who will be sacrificed...
given freely at such a high price...
standing slumped within pride...
dreams crash broken in the sky...
turning from knowledge...
ignoring the cost...
laying to rest...
things not yet lost...
distancing heart from acts of trust...
throwing love under the bus...
round the bend it begins...
tears fall as rust...
darkness closing in...
flames lick wounds...
psyche recoils...
familiar pattern... self-destruct...
refuse to play...
this tired old game...
two step no more...
its lost its hold...
smile.. be bold...
I'm in control...
laugh as ghosts...
spiral out into the cold...
eternal flame burns...
engulfing the broken...
making whole...
my story's told!!!
BY: MAJESTICLADY

FADE TO BLACK

Such a glimmer of hope
From the words he spoke
An unspoken facade
Made her believe
Wishing
Hoping
Praying
That they could be
Blinded
Nearsighted
No colors to see
Cold
Lonely
Misfortunate
Destitute
Maybe something rude
Love was once but a memory
In bedded in the grain
Her eyes show the pain
The bruises deep within
Covering the sin
Tears pour down her cheeks
like faucets they do leak
Heartache
So many mistakes
For loves sake
It's gone
But never forgotten
Dead on arrival
Must be for survival
Can't take it back
Time to fade to black!!!

BY: MS.FOXXXY

*F*ANTASIZED

A storm is brewing...
As kissing takes place, lightning strikes in the same space...twice as the wind arise. Tappings from the rain landing on the window pain, cause a rhythm as we alleviate our clothing. Heart rates increase, beating fast as the thunder begins to roll. Fingertips slowly expediting tingling are across enchanting lands, mesmerized by body language...
My ship begins to sail, causing waves in your sea of enchantment...I stroke like rowing paddles. I feel ur wetness cum down, like a tropical rainstorm, winds at a high speed velocity got us holding on to each other. I see us in the eye of storm. Forces of nature rising. For every push and grind I give, a crack of thunder responds. Imprints of light teeth marks outlining your neck. Tornadoes forming along the horizon, circling all emotions brought forth... A storm that came so perfect and for all that it was worth!!!

BY: THIS1REAL

A storm is brewing...
My heart races to the beat of yours, so close to the eye of the perfect storm. As you kiss my lips, I sigh, outside in the rain, making love on the open terrain, exchanging thunderous winds, lightning strikes, it's time to begin. I need to feel your presence from within, sail off into my port, export my juices, with your tongue, drink me up, let me climb on the highest mountain, let me peak, make it difficult for me to speak, raise up my feet, bring me to ecstasy. Our naked flesh drenched with the rain of our own sweat, as our bodies collide, as the storm takes tide, rippling waves, bring new meaning as your mounting me. Our passion, brings complete satisfaction, when thunder and lightning meet, it brings out the perfect heat!!!

BY: MS.F0XXXY

*F*ANTASIZED *D*AYDREAMS

It wasn't your handsome look..
Or the fact,
that you smelled so good..
That moved me so much.
It was your intellect..
That I could not forget (you)...
Has me longing for your touch.
To feel your hands caressing my thighs...
As you look into my eyes...
Moving in motion to the sway of my hips.
Slow dancing to a sensuous melody...
Body's in unison-in harmony...
I tremble from the warmth of your lips...
Sighing from each kiss.
As I hold you close...
Your manhood lets me know...
It's love in the making...
You will not be forsakened...
As I surrender...
I'm yours for the taking.
I don't plead...
Fulfill this dire need...
Come deep inside of me.
Passionate screams...
You're the man of my dreams...
Here is my heart,
the deed,
and the key.
I will be your woman for all seasons...
Insecureties-I will give no reason...
To ever doubt.
My love & loyalty,
you will never go without...
As tears come to my eyes...

I realize...
I yearn it all to come true.
That happenstance...
That coincidence...
To seize the chance.
My heart yen's...
Cause that what fantasizing does to you!!!
BY: TRANQUIL AMOR

When we crossed paths,
you left a lasting impression.
It was more than just your beauty,
Smile
Shape and
Complexion
I can't even explain,
how you infiltrated my brain
Having visuals of us making love in the rain.
If I could just hold you,
I would never let you go.
Secure you in my love,
and I will always let it show.
Giving you my all
Unconditionally
With consistency
Spontaneous adventures
Intimate evenings by candle lit dinners.
Wrapped in mink fur blankets during long cold winters.
Passionate writings on the walls of your heart.
Engraved with my kisses,
applied to each body part.
Loving you would be a dream come true
But it's a figment of my imagination,
cause that what daydreamers do!!!
BY: THIS1REAL

*F*EELING
(WORDPLAY)

Dark

Shadows

Tears

Overflowing

Heart Breaking

Forever Aching

Pain Soaring

Guard Lowered

Hands Together

Praying Forever

Give Up Never!!!

BY: ATLANTAMOODY

FIRST BLUSH

Walking alone against the wind,

as it's always been…

me against the world…

in the distance I can see someone waving to me…

urging me forward step by step,

strength in his hands,

praise on his lips,

increasing my pace as hope is born…

maybe this is who I've been searching for…

finally before I even realize,

there he stands looking in my eyes,

taking my hand,

shy as can be,

not a word spoken,

too shy to speak,

hearing the truth in the surrounding hush,

together we share our first blush!!!

BY: MAJESTICLADY

Floating From Day To Day

Floating from day to day...

Night comes, and then quickly fades.

Do I even sleep, when I close my eyes...

No rest, no matter how hard I try.

Mind never shuts down...

Wheels constantly spinning 'round.

I no longer dream...

I get flashes of my reality in fast-forward scenes.

Always waking with a jolt...

Damn, I gotta hold... Of my life!

Fuck this strife!

Refuse to be anguished by these worries...

Always in a hurry!

Always thirsting...

Always hurting!

Got too much on my plate...

While helping others balance their weight.

Carrying so much on my back...

Needy & Greedy need to cut me some slack!

Before I really start trippin & flippin...

Yea, I know I'm bitchin...

But can't see my well run dry,

from other muthafucka's dippin!

Got me over thinking...

THE FIRM DIVAS

Over working my psyche,

to keep my ship from sinking.

Gonna start pulling rank...

Start making fools walk the plank.

It's over-due time to alleviate,

alot of this dead weight.

Been going on too long...

Shame on me, for doing myself wrong.

The dunce cap is off...

And enough is enough.

Floating from day to day...

Allowing my dreams to slip away.

No, not anymore!

Gonna rectify this situation...

Steel-toe boot some asses,

then take a past-due vacation.

BY: TRANQUIL AMOR

FORGIVENESS

I Prayed for this.
Defines a true word of assist.
Anybody can make amends.
It shows where true character is.
God forgave us for our sin.
He gave me blessings with a pen.
This is real and not pretend.
We not clanging to differences.
But rejoicing where our passion is.
Poet ac do it B.I.G.
Believe In GOD... till my life end.
Forgiveness for love and friends.
I'm real with mine there's no pretend.
For the right Of flow I will go in.
So if you do not comprehend.
I'll show you so you'll understand...
I'm not perfect I'll never be.
I took what was my penelty.
Just to show that I'm a human being.
And what this friendship means to me.
I'm strong when it means loyalty.
Sometimes the pain can pay the fee.
Before I cast to where it's beef.
The first person I blame is me.
No this is true so now believe.
I wear my heart on my sleeve.
I hope for all to succeed.
With every blood that my heart beats.
Blessed that God forgave me.
And guide me through insanity.
Forgiveness Is beauty
So now I let the world see!!!
BY: POETICACTHEWRITER

THE FIRM DIVAS

Forgivness is where the healing begin,
love thy enemy, will heal sin,
It will save the heart from becoming cold,
God will bless you to fold,
Tired of the wasted anger,
all it does is bring on danger,
a reseloution to find a soultion,
not to perpetuate a disaster,
Got to be a laster,
A leader takes a stand,
families fight, friends fight,
old flames somtimes will ignite,
It's time to stop the madness,
all this does is bring on sadness,
look not to your soul, remember what God says,
and please put beef to bed,
if I can forgive all that's happened to me why can't everybody?
BY: MS.F0XXXY

F*CK*N PERFECT

[Remix To Pink]

Made a lot of mistakes in my life…
Through blood sweat and tears,
I always persevere,
Dissed,
Downgraded
Degenerate,
Made to have felt less than perfect…
Battered,
Maltreated,
Cuffed,
And complicated…
But I know that I'm
Still around…

Fuck saying please,
I'll never again let anyone let me feel less than perfect,
I'm telling myself; I won't let anyone tell me that I'm nothing,
Because everyone who breathes has something to give,
And I'm fucking perfect I'm me…

So sad I let myself feel that I'm unworthy to find love,
That from my past I should be alone,
Shit, no more listening to the voices inside me that tell me,
I don't belong,
That I'm not strong,
Time to be happy,
I've earned my stripes,
unassailable,
noticeable,
Iron like,
Fighting all of those demons in me…

THE FIRM DIVAS

Fuck saying please,
I'll never again let anyone let me feel less than perfect,
I'm telling myself; I won't let anyone tell me that I'm nothing,
Because everyone who breathes has something to give,
And I'm fucking perfect I'm me…

The worlds scared of a woman like me,
What I can do and who I can be,
I can change things,
Done looking at the haterz,
Because they will always be there,
With something to say,
Because when they are unhappy,
They need to look within their hearts,
And ask why?
What about me make me be?

Fuck saying please,
I'll never again let anyone let me feel less than perfect,
I'm telling myself; I won't let anyone tell me that I'm nothing,
Because everyone who breathes has something to give,
And I'm fucking perfect I'm me…

Fuck you if you dont like my look,
dont like my words,
who are you any way...

Fuck saying please,
I'll never again let anyone let me feel less than perfect,
I'm telling myself; I won't let anyone tell me that I'm nothing,
Because everyone who breathes has something to give,
And I'm fucking perfect I'm me…

BY: MS.F0XXXY

FREEDOM

You set me free. once upon a time I was a terrified little girl in a woman's world, a prisoner within myself, scared of the world and even myself... I don't know how or exactly when - you somehow found me in this shell of what was called my life! You saw me buried in the mire and muck , I could not even look up! Beneath the exterior body you entered my mond and saw the real me... the person bound in selfish pity and so much pain....Your compassion wax heartfelt and kindness beyond human giving....God blessed me with an Angel of all angel's to free me to be a woman of God, an effort of an army and the Love of a man combined to set a free a friend in need... Indeed your my hero and you will always have my heart... I don't know if you know how much you gave me... but freedom is not given it is achieved!!!

BY: TONICE

FREEDOM WITHIN

The freedom that lies within me I can't explain it.
Freedom to walk, freedom to sing, freedom to answer a call as it rings
There is a freedom of new beginnings, divorcing the past behind
There is freedom in wounds that miraculously heal over time
The freedom to laugh at things that once made you cry.
The freedom in moving forward and telling past failures good bye
There is freedom in telling yourself that you can succeed
There is freedom in helping those that are in need
The freedom that is liberating the very core of my soul
That freedom is beckoning and commanding me to be whole
There is freedom in not being a slave to anyone or yourself
There is freedom in rebuking demons that try to bring harm or death
The freedom of a fortified place to rest and abide
The freedom in knowing that whatever you go through, God is at your side
Freedom cried, freedom smiled, divine strength given to go an extra mile
Freedom may mean different things for you and me
Freedom is the ability to walk, to move, to see, to be, to progress,
to build, to expand, to forgive........ The song says: I just got to
be free... free.... free........
Thank God for freedom that no man can give or take away....
Praise Our Lord for the liberty we have today.....
Freedom from guilt and sin......
FREEDOM WITHIN!!!

BY: CARAMELCAKE54

GET TO STEPPING

I stuck to my vows,

I'll send you packin without a kiss,

what once was a dream

only was a nightmare.

we wasn't a team.

you got your own;

thanks you left me alone

the night you left,

you thought I'd die but guess what

I didn't even cry.

see the curb that's where you should be,

yeah I'm disturbed, crazy you said?

oh well.

My life is much better without you cause my love for you is dead!

BY: DARKANGEL68

GYPSYSTORM

Gypsy dancing round the flame...

seductive eyes,

saucy hips,

laughter wild and free,

storm raging on the horizon,

she dances fearlessly,

fluid grace harmonious aura of confidence,

smiling knowingly gazing into souls,

reflective primitive beauty every dip and sway,

a story upon her lips,

magical steps

spiritual power in her song

a tale as old as time itself!!!

BY: MAJESTICLADY

HAPPINESS OVER SADNESS

I choose happiness over sadness any day
Emotional feelings
taken over so it's no time to play
I want to believe that your love for me is here to stay
But once again I'm force to choose
Happiness over sadness
Pain is something that you make me feel each day
it would be easy if I just run away
No one should have to put up with what I been thru
You always telling me what to do
I'm grown just like you
You raise your fist
And you think beating me is worth the risk
Black eyes and busted lips
Following down with my cloths ripped
Come on let me give you a tip
All this fighting is over
Believe me it's time to dip
Don't come looking for me
because it would be a wasted trip
That was one of the hardest decisions
To choose my happiness over sadness!!!

BY: ATLANTAMOODY

*H*ARD *T*IMES

Times are hard everywhere you look around and turn.
Economic disaster has seemed to hit every home in return.

The cries of single moms are heard by near neighbors.
Trying tenaciously to make ends meet is worse than labor.

The cry of a child that hasn't enough to eat.
The ridicule he receives at school, about the shoes on his feet.

The frustration of a man not being able to hold his own.
Reflections of his past haunt him in seeds that were sown.

People doing things that they never imagined they would do.
Compromising their integrity just to get through.

Families fighting and arguing with many demeaning shouts.
Resenting having to wait and be called for a government handout.

Dysfunction on the rise, heavy crime creating demise.
The love of many waxing cold is no surprise.

Bitterness against a society as a whole.
Dreams shattered that were untold.

Opportunity knocking on the doors of some and not on others.
Distance and defeat separating lovers.

Hard times are everywhere you look around and turn.
Stand strong and don't allow this economic crisis to burn!!!

BY: CARAMELCAKE54

HE LOVES ME, HE LOVES ME NOT

He loves me,
he loved me not,
I was stunned and divested
on how he treated me on our last days.
Yes-every now and then I get flashbacks,
because how wrong he did me was whack.

He loves me,
he loved me not
though we were together for short period of time
I've learned and seen alot of revelations right in front of my face.
The shit was going on so fast It felt like a rat race,
so I promised myself no more pain
and tears caused from him.

He loves me,
he loved me not,
he was full of bs,
did nothing but give me
anger and grief at the end.
I thought there was true love one time with him,
but once it's said & done all things
that were said to me became lies,
and a bullshit ass talk.
He did nothing,
but put on a smoke screen,
and fake ass pipe dreams.
Because in reality, he didn't love me.

He loved me, he loved me not!!!

BY: LAVENDER LADY

HOME

North, South, East, West… where oh where do the wanders go...
Why not zig than zag, why not try till home feels right?
Everyone thinks they know, but no one really does-life is a puzzle and the
picture is not clear till it is done.
People want to force the pieces to fit but they don't and won't because it was
not meant to be-simply not a match to each.
Winds blow, sun radiates and birds fly, but noone can reach the heights the
birds flies without the help of a machine...
Birds do it naturally and gracefully.
Ride the wind as it blows the life North, South, East, West… settling in the
nest that is called home!
Time to explore and adore the gifts of Mother Nature and her handy work.
Everyone wants to be the one chosen, but jealousy and anger are aroused...
when not picked, but noone has taken the time to be a friend and enjoy the
gifts without expectations or insecurities.... why not let God choose?
Friends first and last no matter who or what happens!!!

BY: TONICE

HOPE

If hope springs eternal
then what happens
when the well runs dry?

You search everywhere
for that one thing
that makes you believe the life living.

When hope for the future
is obscured by memories of the past,
all that you do is a calculated move.
One mistake and all hope is lost.

A voice inside you says,
"There is always hope!"
Even when you lose faith,
somehow you know in your gut there is hope.

This isn't a new age concept,
hope has always been here.
Through time and memorial
hope comes out of darkest hours.

BY: DARKANGEL68

HOUSE OF THE DEVIL

Today I sat in the house of the devil,
home plate,
abandoned hope,
at the charcoal gate.
A fiery glare from inside this cell,
a ice cold grip of fear,
lamenting cries,
deafening my ears.
A crooked little grey house,
teetering between two hills,
a garden of weeds,
Venus fly traps for thrills.
A short dusty path,
to the front door,
Shoes caked in the mud and blood,
of the enslaved unsaved poor.
The smell of sulfur,
wafting the stale air,
upon a rickety porch,
rocks an unsteady chair.
The door slightly opens,
heavy with a creeeeeeeek,
"Don't go in!!!"
all the garden begins to shreek.
My heart slows,
thudding harder and harder,
as I hear the drip and drip,
of the rusted faucet water.
"Fancy a cup my sweet little dear?"
I turn up my nose,
my face twisted in a jeer,
as the cup is trusteed to my lips,
a sharp smell of death,

as the devil slowly sips.
"Hair of the dog,, maybe the cat."
The door slams behind me,
"a little of this, maybe that."
the smell of maggots burns every word,
"Get comfy my dear, dont be absurd.
This right here my love, is your new world."
Blinking my eyes,
reality sets in,
Heaven was my battle,
the devil my sin.
Now keep your house,
for there is no mistaking,
for the devils house isn't about escaping!!!

BY: ARTICHOKEHEART

I Love It When

I love it when you say I LOVE YOU.
I love it when you call me baby.
This may sound corny,
but I don't care because love is in the air.
and the air we share is pure and beautiful - so fruitful.
I love it when you make laugh, or smile, it makes me feel you were Heaven-
sent.
Every time I hear your lovely and handsome voice...
I get breathless, hardly any words to say, it makes me speechless.
I love it when you talk about our future - and you say it's my heart you want
to nurture, and I'm going to do the same.
One day we will have the same last name.
I love it when you stop my mind from going back into the past, and tell me to
move forward,
because I have him as a better man now, and even loves my son like his own.
I love it when you say sweet nothings, or naughty things in my ear.
I love it when
the fact that you have a caring soul, which satisfy mines.
I love the respect you have for me as your woman, as your friend, as a
person, a human being!
I love it when I feel that you're right here with me.
The good thing about it, is we'll see each other soon...
But for now, like my girl Alicia Keys say's,
THROUGH DISTANCE IN TIME, I'LL BE WAITING!!!

BY: LAVENDER LADY

I SENSE

This is the last call, before I fall,
but don't worry yall, arms are out to catch me,
and wrap me up in heavenly,
Summers bliss, in his kiss,
heat index on the rise,
as he caresses me with his eyes,
the succulent scan of my thighs,
his sight lingers upon the prize,
but then all of a sudden he is blind,
strong hands become his mind,
following the soft curves I am outlined,
and these fingers dip and wind,
but just as quick he cannot feel,
the peak of perfection is just to real,
so his tongue now becomes the wheel,
tasting deeper into appeal,
tracing unexploreable lands,
too soft and gentle for rough hands,
too enticing for just mere sight,
where only taste buds can work just right,
he hits that spot with a slight swirl,
it starts with G, cause honestly,
that's what it takes to get that pearl,
eyes of an angel and hands of a saint,
but a portrait of heaven is all his tongue can paint,
he has won with all his charm,
two become one within soft walls of disarm,
and the soft smell of pleasure lingers in the air,
and the sweet whispers of moans still ringing in our ears,
But the feel of passion and the touch of heat,
is on repeat, it will never end,
cause feelings always remain when you take your lover who was your friend!!!

BY: ARTICHOKEHEART

I SHOULD KNOW BETTER

I have 10 minutes-
make that 5!!!
So let me say this fast..
Or so I'll try. Vent..
Repent..
Mami went through a small snap.
Had to get my mind back..
Veering a lil' off track.
Life can make ya go through that..
But I'm back. Stand up..
Man up..
Had to remind myself.
Do what I gotta do..
It ain't about nobody else.
Get right within..
Nobody has to live in this skin.
Get act like a loser, still expecting to win.
So I lifted my head up high..
Let all the bullshit fly..
Got my eyes back on the prize.
Unconcerned with trivial mess..
I should know better-
I'm too blessed, to be stressed.
Gave the nonsense over..
Reclaiming my happiness.
Peace to my Fam' & Diva Sisters!!!

BY: TRANQUIL AMOR

I Wanna Be Loved

Love is an emotional bonding
Your feeling are responding
To the attraction you have for someone
I wanna be loved…
Rubbed
Kissed
And hugged
I need to feel that emotional tie
I can't lie
I wanna be loved…
It's more than about making love
Or having someone sharing your bed each night
Each day I'm out there fighting fight after fight
Trying to get that love some people have taken for granted
But their just enchanted
With the idea of being with someone
Playing with others feeling so to me my fight is never done
I wanna be loved…
Adored
Cherish
Explored
Is it too late for me to find my true love
God I hope not in time I'll get my answer from above
I'm a good woman and I work hard and easily loved
Would someone ever take the time to see me for who I am
I don't know but what I'm saying is a fact
When that special person do walk into my life
they will never want to go back
My good and loving spirit would attack
Shining on them with all I have to offer
Why…
I wanna be loved!!!

BY: ATLANTAMOODY

IF I HAD WINGS

If I had wings,

I'd give you that of which ur heart sings,

among other things,

like where we both rockin rings,

but i=I don't and it fkn stings,

for if I had wings I'd fly to your side many yesterday's ago,

I'd hold you tight as the tears would flow,

whisper I love you and never let go,

with my wings I'd wipe your final tear,

"baby I'm here,

"you've got nothin more to fear,

but I'm only human-which comes with limitations,

and everyday complications,

and gotdamn da frustrations!!

I try to be strong,

cause I'm so away from you is where I don't belong,

for in you, my heart has already found its home!!!

BY: L4DY B

In The Blind

So easy for a pebble to turn into a boulder,
a lot harder to brush the world off your shoulder,
so many things to make you look wrong,
what's the point of being right,
living life by broken rules all along,
you can't trust anything in sight,
yet blindness is a handicap,
that I don't understand,
all other senses used for crap,
and this one isn't so grand,
we can't see in front of our faces,
fallen stars and bitter angels,
heavenly disgraces,
and love it distorts and tangles,
the blistering bliss,
of that stinging kiss,
what ignorance is this,
the blind ones diss,
that's why mountains never bend,
and water never breaks,
why the blind never pretend,
to know what seeing takes!!!

BY: ARTICHOKEHEART

IN TOTAL BLISS

My love
Mi amor
As I gaze at you through
A closed curtain
Only to reveal a vague silhouette
You relentlessly and courageously
Keep advancing near
Rejecting all caution
All lights about you
Are burning bright
Gallantly announcing to the world
My love comes...
I have nothing to hide
Warm loving embrace
The vital signs are so impossible
To misread
Reject not....
The passionate cry of my heart
To ignore all these impulses
Would totally be preposterous
In action like a school boy
I claim you and so demand
YOU....
Be mine
And finally
My love....let this puzzle
Fall in place and be solved!!!
BY: PURE ECHO PLAY

As my heart hide behind a covered shield
Thoughts and feelings connect and reveal
Not underestimating my affection but

THE FIRM DIVAS

Allowing love to have a projection
A vision that's crystal clear, not opaque
Willful love that's no mistake
Acknowledging the signs that are written on the wall...of my heart
Beautiful start... I must say
You not turning away... but bringing hope on my rainy day
I'm open like a book without a riddle
Straight shots singing to the tune of a fiddle
Reading each other right, having futuristic foresight
My heart cries with passion as well
Solutions to verbalize, feel and tell
Mi amor my love
Come closer to me...As I submit to your embrace
Claiming us as winners in each of our eyes
Receiving the prize of being loved... by YOU
Solving the mystery... I'm Yours!!!

BY: CARAMELCAKE54

IT'S BUT A MERE TOOL

It's not something I idolize..
When I see other's with more than I have-
I don't despise..
Envy & greed, is not my drive.
It just inspires me to strive.
It can never make me a fool..
To survive, I know the rules..
It's but a mere tool..

To get what I need - materialistically, I speak.
It cannot make me weak..
Causing me to commit an act of ignorance..
To suffer the penalty of consequence.
It's but a mere tool..

That only has but a bit of control..
Never can it cause me to sacrifice my soul.
For what I truly seek, is
not the pie in the sky..
There are no stars in these eyes..
I seek eternal life.
So, no, it's not what I idolize..
It's but a mere tool, to survive.
Paper, cheddar, Benjamin's..
Whatever you call it - ya can't take it with you, in the end!!!

BY: TRANQUIL AMOR

IVORY QUEEN

At times I feel nothing is different,
fighting the same war,
just with different armies.
My life a map of battlefields,
and no soldiers of love.
Lieutenant to heartbreak,
a commander of none.
Growing weary on the frontline,
and the enemy has won.
Sometimes I almost feel robotic,
shooting off the same gun,
a machine of locks and loads,
but never being drawn.
A vast universe of Neptune,
and I'm the only sun,
beating down from heaven,
the day has just begun.
My spirit swiftly broken,
finding differences amongst the same,
the broken queen glued together,
seems like fairer game.
My knight has fallen, taken by the moon,
I believe I have a calling,
to move along too soon.
But I desire not, for a war time rook,
to spoil the throne for my king,
on some ebony crook.
The ivory tears of a queen,
my cardboard kingdom shook,
in times of peace, or in war,
love is sought,
but where to look!!!

BY: ARTICHOKEHEART

JUST ONE OF THEM DAYZ

(To Him)
Wit you I felt da connection from da start,
see I was dead, but you was da resurrection of my heart,
me and you boo was like perfection, neva thought we'd part,
but through my dreams you threw a dart,
they say love is blind but sweety I ain't,
I could tell you was no saint,
always gotta flirt,
out doin your dirt,
wasn't thinkin bout me and how it hurt,
1st I was devastated,
till I seen you fkn wit da same bitch "Kevin" dated,
my how you've downgraded,
I don't want nothin 2 do wit you if you hit dat,
you can have her and da std's that come wit dat...

(To Her)
Bitch you a nasty hoe,
trashy though,
dick riding my man since 4eva,
a dirty bitch you knew we was togetha,
postn pix of ya fatass up on his page,
thinkin you cute when you look like you should be in a cage,
disrespectin me sweety you on da wrong stage,
this A DIVA show,
not da story of da sideline hoe,
ya ass needa go,
all 311 pounds of ya needa get to kickin rocks,
dudes ratha stick they dik n sox,
but I mean if ol' boy want you he can have you, I'll let em leave,
cause best believe,
afta touchin you he ain't fkn wit my beev,
dat's a whole notha level of decieve,

THE FIRM DIVAS

bitch your pubes as nappy as ya weave,
ya you betrayed me,
an dude played me,
but baby,
if he fukn wit you, he crazy,
nah I ain't sad,
and nah I ain;t mad,
in fact I feel 4 him, he downgraded hella bad!!!

BY: L4DY B

LAST STAND

Black blood seeps beneath my nails,
welts across neck and back,
bruises lay darkly across my cheeks,
madness rattles round my brain,
hatred leaves its stain,
where once there stood a child with dreams,
there stands an icy angry vengeful Queen,
drawing upon sources unknown,
a call to war as foretold,
battle armor placed upon this once innocent heart,
sword and shield,
lance and bow,
take no prisoners,
KILL THEM ALL!!!
Burn their houses while they sleep,
leave no trace of their plight,
they don't deserve to go down in history,
erase their names from The Book Of Life,
send their souls fleeing into hell-fire,
demons' names never known, faces,
hearts made of stone,
chisel in my name lest they forget,
hell can never conquer this glorious daughter of the King,
laughter bounces off the hills,
wild and free,
warrior cries echo within,
firey heart, golden soul,
any that care to see,
this wasteland of misery's last gasp,
last hold, after today,
it shall be no more!!!BY:

MAJESTICLADY

LOST IN EMOTION

Lost in the emotions of my heart...
hoping you see the love inside me...
the love I can bring...
if only for the spring...
I had a dream last night..
we made love on the beach...
we held each other for dear life...
I was more than your lover I was your wife...
our bodies sung a song so deep...
so in tune...
it's like when the flowers bloom...
eternity was you and me...
we looked up at the first star and made a wish...
than we sealed it with a kiss...
so long and soulful...
destiny holds me tonight...
wishing we would be alright...
he stared at me as I began to cry and said baby if its Gods plan...
you and me will run free...
through the meadows...
making love on a bed of rose pedals...
hold on to this dream of you and me for eternity...
I'm lost in the emotions of this dream...
hoping that our love can be what it seemz!!!

BY: MS.F0XXXY

Lost Innocence

(A DIVA SUMMIT ON CHILD ABUSE)

• *It is estimated that between 60-85% of child fatalities due to maltreatment are not recorded as such on death certificates.*

• *90% of child sexual abuse victims know the perpetrator in some way; 68% are abused by family members.*

• *Child abuse occurs at every socioeconomic level, across ethnic and cultural lines, within all religions and at all levels of education.*

- *Children are suffering from a hidden epidemic of child abuse and neglect.*
  Over 3 million reports of child abuse are made every year in the United States; however, those reports can include multiple children.

- *In 2007, approximately 5.8 million children were involved in an estimated 3.2 million child abuse reports and allegations...*

A child is brought into the world is supposed to be loved, cherished and protected...
It is said it takes a village to raise a child, but then the child is hurt, nelgelated or even tortured
Physically, mentally, emotionally always damaging them spiritually...
Why do so many villagers turn a blind eye to what they see happening daily?
A child dies at the hands of family member that was the one entrusted through n through
The scars seen in many adult behaviors that where from early childhood terrors...
Foundations of our future intertwined with fear, hate, and lust....
Why do we keep turning away and blaming everybody and doing nothing ourselves?

Are we not responsible for protecting a stranger as well?
Trust is gone and these little people grow and walls go up and they do what
they do to deal with the results of an uncle or neighbor taking away
their innocence or their primary caregiver beating them senseless...
Trust never given root and love gone unseen...
Is it any wonder the cycle continues and they do to other children as was
done to them...
Is it supposed to just disappear because it is wrong...
Do we have the obligation or responsibility to change this wrong or shut our
eyes and just let it go on!!!
BY: TONICE

It's sad to hear how a lot of children get abused by parents.

Sometimes I wonder to myself,
what's the point in having children if they aren't going to do right by them.
I'm glad I have a mother who actually guides me and makes it known when
wrong or right
but don't unnecessarily put hands on me just for the hell of it.
A real parent would give you tough love, discipline, teach you from their
experiences,
and will tell don't follow their footsteps.
Real parents would want what's best for you,
not abusing you.
So for the parents who is raising their children the correct,
and caring way,
I have much love and props for you, but as for the ass holes fathers,
and bitches for mothers I discriminate your asses!!!
BY: LAVENDER LADY

   • *A report of child abuse is made every ten seconds.*

   • *Almost five children die every day as a result of child abuse. More
   than three out of four are under the age of 4. to be cont....*

THE FIRM DIVAS

Ah, the 'Rosy Front'... Seems the children have everything they want. Get whatever they ask for.. But it's sad, what goes on behind closed doors. Material possessions are not enough, to compensate for the lack of love. Money can't buy bliss... Only superficial happiness... To keep things quiet, a trinket, is but a quick-fix. Parents put up a facade, to hide their misery.

To keep up the, 'Rosy Front', for society. Who's deaf, dumb & blind, or refuses to hear or see... The sadness in a child's eyes, or any other obvious signs. A child withdrawn or cold... Snotty or spoiled, is the reason told.

More money, more ways to hide abuse. It only happens in the ghetto, is the biggest untruth. Pay close attention to the news... Kids from the 'hood', is labeled gangstas & no good. That's what they shout! It's the kids, 'well to do', that take each other& thier parents out. They don't just suddenly snap! Fall for that- fall for crap!

Abuse has no monetary value. It happens everywhere, and that's the raw truth! Behind that 'Rosy Front' is alot of dirt.. Psychological, Emotional, & Physical hurt.. And you wonder why, Joe Blow, came from riches, now lives on skid row. Or why Susie Q, talks to herself, doing what she do... Using drugs to numb her, to escape reality, of painful memories...

Being beat with the buckle of a belt. Cause of the 'rosy front', society overlooked thier hell.. Now they're grown, and all alone. Being looked upon as a waste... The real disgrace is child abuse. Children don't ask to be born... Let alone, into the hands of misuse. To be that punching bag, when it's all bad... It's so sad. With tears, I lift my eyes... Father, let not another child suffer or meet an untimely demise. I ask that you rectify, a sickness, that's destroyed many innocent lives!!!!

BY: TRANQUIL AMOR

Lil girl lost in a world so cold,
only has herself if the truth be told,
years of lies,
seeing tears in her mother's eyes,
Daddy's gone never to be seen again,
Clothes tattered and torn,
A girl who wishes she was never born,

THE FIRM DIVAS

A life caught up without any grace,
lost and hungry without a place,
People see her but they don't ask why,
cause if they did the truth might make them cry....

Lil girl lost no place to call home,
Living the life that she didnt choose,
poor lil angel so abused,
A mother who don't see what's in front of her face,
bringing strangers,
such a disgrace...

Lil girl lost so drenched in fear,
sometimes wishing someone would just see her tear!!!
BY: MS.F0XXXY

Children grow up so fast
Most don't have a mom or dad
Hiding behind their-self
Most don't even care
They turn to sex and drugs
While their parents push what they're seeing under the rug
And we wonder how our children turn out this way
Most kids are alone day after day
What some parents are doing is giving the kids clothing, food to eat,
and a place to stay
It's sad what the world is coming to
Most parent try to be their kids friends now tell me what that's gonna prove
Parent continue having kids putting the new ones on the older ones
When their done rising their brothers and sister they not gonna even one

THE FIRM DIVAS

I see this every day
The sad and hurt looks in some kids faces
The things that goes on behind closed doors
Some kids leave him early so they can put the responsibly but on the
parents now that's a way to settle the score.
I can go on and on how our kids lost their innocence
But to me it just doesn't make any sense!!!
BY: ATLANTAMOODY

Many talk of others loss of innocence,
what about your own,
sucked slowly from your essence,
the marrow to your bone,
slowly at the world's expense,
you become alone.

Viewing the world as a fantasy,
So gigantic and oh so grand,
and underlying ecstasy,
to everybody's hand,
but one day you wake to complacency,
and you assimilate to understand.

Tribulations and trials,
losing the fantasy bit by bit,
finding mountains made of piles,
amongst tat for tit,
shrinking minutes from long whiles,
preaching from a pulpit.

THE FIRM DIVAS

Reality sets in,
and there is no turning back,
a hand slipping over you in sin,
seeing all that you lack,
watching the end begin,
just to keep you on track.

The end is near,
this is the new age,
innocence takes up the rear,
in the form of an old sage,
fighting to pass on to a new year,
but losing to a turning page.

Generations becoming less and less,
a sign of the times,
I becomes lost in the mess,
of subliminal sublimes,
dulling the moral compass,
to keep up with guilty rhymes.

This is my loss,
my burden to hold,
bore upon a cross,
one I will carry to get to the throne,
fading against this world,
but my innocence in heaven had always shone!!!
BY: ARTICHOKEHEART

THE FIRM DIVAS

Most of the people we see don't want to live in a shelter and feel safe in their own little camp.
Experience has taught me that almost 100 percent of these people suffered abuse as children.
Well over half have emotional, mental problems. Most have drug and alcohol problems.
BY: John Gallagher

I was angry about the fact that my father would beat my mother on a daily basis,
that my mother would take it in turn and beat on me.
I was an abused child. I was mad about all those things, very bitter and very angry.
BY: Rick James R.I.P

Although the world is full of suffering, it is full also of overcoming it.
BY: Helen Keller R.I.P

A lot of people in our community don't want to believe that child abuse happens in their neighborhoods — but it does.
BY: Shari Pulliam

In my view, there is nothing more vicious and outrageous than the abuse, exploitation and harm of the most vulnerable members of our society, and I firmly believe that our nation's laws and resources need to reflect the seriousness of these terrible crimes.
BY: Bob Ney

PLEASE THIS IS A WORLD WIDE PROBLEM!
it really does take a village to raise a child.
When you see a child in trouble please do something please report it!!!

THE FIRM DIVAS

LOVE

builds u up, breaks u down, claws incessantly at ur heart, makes u a queen or a clown, takes over ur mind from the start, leaves u full of life and laughter, takes u to hell forever after, mankind has chased this entity calling it blind, a decision, prison, saying it sets ur true self free....leaves u twisting in the wind, no shelter from its closest kin, passionate, firey romanticized lust, leaves u wounded, lying in the dust,...lifts ur spirits, flight of a dove, this gift from god, this thing called love, make u crazy, make u sane, leave u crying all alone, sharpest weapon ever known....sheathed in gentle admiration, sharpened constantly upon agitation, it's the only thing worth fighting for, brings u peace, causes wars,...love....knocking at ur door, open the gate, set it free, this is the definition of love to me!!!

BY: MAJESTICLADY

Love The Way You Lie

Promised to always be there, yet you desert me,
Said you loved me and would never hurt me,
yet with the same hands you give pleasure you cause pain,
I'm emotionally drained,
No matter how hard I cry,
Still I can't deny,
I fukkin love the way you lie,
The cute lil' faces you make when you do it,
and how you try and stutter your way through it,
like there ain't nothin to it,
you hear my heart call,
an don't seem to care at all,
turn just to watch me fall,
see unlike you I been true from the start,
and when I love its wit my whole heart, Though sometimes I don't love
smart,
I'll admit, sometimes I jump into things to fast,
Put my heart on blast,
and expect the fairy tale shit to last,
But it ended ugly just like my ex,
and it'd probably be the same wit the next, That's why I show no love and
only in it for the sex,
Use to believe in love now I don't,
Use to fall for lies, but now I won't,
It was a harsh lesson to learn,
But since you like to play wit fire I'ma let you burn!!!

BY: L4DY B

LOVES EVENT

Romance is a dish,

that's best served hot.

Exploration of your body,

in search of the right spot.

Passion filled kisses that could ignite a bonfire.

We illuminated the skies with the expression of one's desire.

Destination: Loveland, our palace waits.

Ecstasy leads us in the direction of Euphoria.

No longer in need to search with it being at the tips of our fingers.

Understanding the unknown and bringing it into sight.

If love is blind,

How could it be our guiding light?

I found you and You found me but love found we.

Such a beautiful connection.

My fingers in your hair while ur stroking my erection.

With our lips locked and our tongues beginning to wrestle.

The lighting from the candle flickers

Because we're breathing so intense.

This intimate setting has me convinced that we are meant.

This is more than just a happening, this is Loves Event!!!

BY: THIS1REAL

THE FIRM DIVAS

It happened by surprise,

Can't believe I seen the look in your eyes,

Loves first dawn,

New like a baby fawn,

Such a beautiful connection,

Lost in the desire of the moment.

Our lips touched and,

The magic began,

A new test of time,

This was our sign,

So intense was our first dance,

It was like we was both in a trance,

Caught in that moment,

Our love was unrit,

The desire to be in your embrace,

Left me lost without a trace,

It was more than words baby,

You was Heaven sent,

This is loves event!!!

BY: MS.FOXXXY

LOVING PASSION

Desires of passion seeping through my veins.
Womanhood being expressed in a sensual way.
Loving with all I have til nothing remains.
Illuminating intimacy under the moon, progressing til the day.
Compassionate caress as we give each other our very best.
Contentment relaxes me as I lay and stroke your chest.
Getting familiar with the fragrance of each of our scents.
Never to be forgotten, as our minds come together and circumvent.
Understanding the need that each of us possess, allows us to willingly give,
with no contest.
Love me like never before, nothing shameful, nothing to abhor.
I believe in reciprocity because it"s fair and I like to give expecting all in
return. Ignited fire, a heart that yearns...for you. Secluded away from
everyday distractions. Relishing each other as a coming attraction. Mmm
Caliente Mi amor padre..twisted tongue not knowing what to say. I love you
papi, you are so hot.... Love me and don't ever stop.... a storm is brewing in
the atmosphere... Hold me tight my love and take away my fear.
The wind is blowing and thrusting upon the windows and walls of our
chamber. Roars of passion without passivity echoes in climatic creativity....
loving me deep, loving you strong.... loving each other all night long!!!

BY: CARAMELCAKE54

MAE

I know it's hard to deal with at your age,
Left wit so many questions and a heart full of rage,
Just take the pen to your page,
And make the world your stage,
You're a beautiful gurl wit so much potential,
so spread you're wings and soar,
when opportunity knocks, answer the door,
Give it all you got, if not more,
Tilt ya head back and roar,
its ok to cry,
But don't let your life pass you by
Waitin on answers as to why,
Some things you may never know,
and from the pain you can only grow,
But never let your weakness show,
Some things are better left unsaid,
so don't fill your head,
Wit what would've been,
What should've been,
Or how could it end,
I been there,
I know you question if she care,
About the bond yall spouse to share,
that you need her but she's never there,
Baby girl, life's never really fair...
But you're strong as I have had to be,
And if you need reassurance take one look at me,
I stood in your shoes,
Ive lived the blues,
But I refused to lose...
Take my hand and I'll help you along the way,
Make sure you never stray,
Remember, there's always a better way,
and tomorrow's another day!!!
BY: L4DY B

MAMA

Living without you, was hard to handle,
Every year as I blew out my bday candle,
It was you I was wishin for,
Heart full of hope in eyes on the door,
Another no show, and that's when the tears would pour...
Another year,
Without you here,
Another tear,
You didn't hear,
Mama, I just wanted you near...
But you were fightin an addiction; tryna gain the upper hand,
you just needed time and I guess I can understand,
In considering the circumstance,
I gave you a second chance...
my Mama, my best friend,
I can't go through this again,
Can you tell me will it ever end??
Can we ever mend,
maybe play pretend!!!

BY: L4DY B

MATURING

I'M MATURING EVEN MORE THAN BEFORE...

I'M STARTING TO SEE MANY THINGS COME TO LIGHT,
THAT I WAS TAUGHT FROM MY MOTHER.

I'M MATURING BECOMING MORE OF A GROWN WOMAN,
INSTEAD OF A YOUNG WOMAN.

I'M MATURING LEARNING WHAT'S VALUABLE,
AND WHAT'S NOT...

AND THATS MY SON!!!

BY: LAVENDER LADY

MARSHELL LAW

If Marshall Law was imposed
And you could not
write not a one poetic verse
No dramatic word play
Just can't do it !
no no no! Its forbidden....

I be the leader of the resistance. I give a fuck about the rules of the few. Lock me up in Guantanamo. I'd gladly scream - Give us US free - Fightin the unjust law in a desolate land. Till my lungs collapse Id cry foul from the mountains peak into the lowest valley. Give me liberty. I declare my independence one verse at a time. Damn the consequence. We'd assemble in tiny candlelit basements snappn fingers over heartfelt expression. My poetry landing me in the slammer. Id bleed for my ink. Fuck Martial and his law... muthafuka gonna need an army to silence me. Poetry is foood for thought and im the buffet. A lil something for everybody. I'd graffiti the world with couplets. Free verse, my mic. This spinnin rock my stage. You can beat me, but u will NEVER defeat my talented page.... Did i just break the law ?
BY: LEO LUV

What?
can't have my song?
No music
No rhyme
This is Anarchy
My heart says this is Blasphamy
Nothing to write with
Now this is a sin
I'd rather die than not rhyme
No flow My headz spinning this is the biginning
New World Order is here WAIT!!!!!
Underground is where I'll go
My wordz are my soul

THE FIRM DIVAS

I will not give up armed only with my paper and pen
I will stand up and fight be ready to defend
I will not give up my SONG!!!
BY: MS.F0XXXY

The year was 1859 and it seemed everybody had gold fever.. And people would come from miles and miles to listen to tales of the story weaver.. See those who heard her poetic narratives would then have luck.. Strike it rich, out in the old west, during the gold rush. But theres a new Marshall in town and hes causing an uproar. Banned all creative flow, similes and metaphors.. Locked up the story weaver and sentenced her to hang.. Now theres roit outside da saloon, and a hush fell over the crowd after a loud BANG.. After that utter chaos, guns a blaze.. People running, looting, fighting, shooting, smoke and dust cause a haze.. Amidst the comotion the storyweaver sat in her lonely jailcell.. Secretly scribbin creative prose and poetry her escape from this hell.. Baffled the Marshall how can she be so calm facin death.. She explain if u take away a person right to express themselves theres nothing left.. She revealed it wasnt her poetry and stories that lead people to find gold ..but that it expands imagination, build

dreams, give folks something to live for.. That life gets hard to deal with,wild and crazy like what was goin on outside.. Sometime folks need to mentally escape, a safe place to hide. They continued to chats, Her words so sincer!!!
BY: GUD GIRL GONE BAD601

So flabbergasted and bewildered
A long sigh........and
My eyes quickly.......
blinked sporadically!
In hopes
I was simply reading
The words wrong

Mind gave me complete
Reasurance and so I
Began aginizing and contemplating
No rymhm!

THE FIRM DIVAS

No expressive word articulation!
Body, mind and soul
On one accord...... immediately
Renounce and bickered
HELL HAH!
Can't do it! not even for a minute
Pow!Pow!
I must bust on da ass

Instantly transformed.....
To a vigilante
Cause poetry
will always be my mistress
In high and low places
Say Say!
I will let my words fly and resonate in the air
With so much balls
Hell ya!
You just tell the law to come on!

With a head butt
Nonchalant blasé blasé
I'm ready
every which away
Always down for some spicy
Word play
Much drama as I work and fineness my words so eloquently!!!
BY: PURE ECHO PLAY

MIRROR, MIRROR

Mirror, mirror o how I hate you sometimes,
Paint a picture so clear,
Of the one thing I fear,
Lookin back is only hurtin me,
Lookin forward n I'm scared of the uncertainty,
Mirror o mirror,
where do I go from here??

The eyes I see,
Staring back at me...
Tell a story without sayin a word,
Unlike any I've ever heard,
A young woman trapped like an unwilling bird...

so much pain in the tears that they cry,
It shows on her face, the dark circles of every unsuccessful try,
On the inside lookin out, waitin on her chance to fly!!

Mirror o mirror, shattered by anger,
Who is this beautiful stranger,
A face broken down into sections,
Each shard displaying its own perfections,
Staring up at me from the ground,
Such pretty eyes so big and round,
What is this that I've found,
A new confidence from within,
A strength that will carry me to the end,
eyes that once carried bags from a girl tryna cope,
and had her lookin like she was on dope,
Now so full of hope...

Full lips that used to frown, now form a smile,
A sight(side) of me I ain't seen in a while,

THE FIRM DIVAS

Mirror o mirror how I thank you...you found a way to remind me,
Broke things down n made it easy to find me,
Released me from the devices that once used to bind me,

Mirror oh mirror how I love you!!
paint a picture so clear,
I've got nothing to fear,
I know now, exactly where to go from here!!!
BY: L4DY B

MOMMA'S BOY

He was just thirteen,
and couldn't understand who was this man,
coming in trying to be his Dad.

He didn't need one,
he walked out and never looked back,
never had anyone to teach him Hacky Sack.

He took care of his mama,
kept her away from drama,
she was his heart,
but now there was this man trying to tear them apart.

Wanting to be his friend,
until the marriage began.
Then he was left out in the cold,
step daddy then started to get bold,
turned mean and cold.

At night he'd hear his Mama cry,
hiding the bruises saying she wanted to die.
Mama's boy's anger stepped in,
this was the biginning of the end.

One night a gun, no more time for fun,
the story didn't end here Mama's boy is doing thirty years.
Every night Mama shed tears,
why did she bring him in,
should've been happy with just her and him!!!

BY: MS. FOXXXY

MOMMA'S WORK IS NEVER DONE

Momma's work is never done.
Get up so early, to wake my kids & the sun.

They're off to school & the sun is shining.
Alone time, is spent pining.

What all do I have to do today...

Check over my schedule
throw myself together,
and I'm on my way.

Handle all my biz.
Gotta get back home, to receive my kids.

It's homework & dinner.

Momma works nights
So it's taken over by the babysitter.

On my days off, I try to sleep in.
No, there's just more time for me to squeeze more errands in.

Yet, if I had the chance to just be lazy
I believe I'd go stir crazy.

My friends ask me, do I ever have fun?
Do I ever take a 'me' day?

I tell them,
You know, Momma's work is never done,
and I wouldn't have it any other way!!!

BY: TRANQUIL AMOR

MOTHERLESS CHILD

Wasn't going to write... can't help myself... one conversation... in love and friendship...uncovered a wound...
I thought was healed... if that was true... I wouldn't feel.. hollow within... tense without... her name echos... like lost screams...
heart breaks... over remembered things... accepting once again... I am among the motherless children...
the emptiness of loss... the void of despair... what's so wrong with me... that she didnt care?...
how did I, her firstborn girl... become her sacrificial lamb?... I wasn't perfect... though I tried at first... I wasn't evil...
I didn't crawl in the dirt... I wasn't special... not on the surface... I wasn't anything... that deserved what I got...
I loved that woman painfully... her hatred was plain to see... bowing, scraping, begging on my knees...
please dear God... make her love me... the love though battered... sometimes lost...
or maybe just the need to be wanted... by the beast that bore me... is still there... else why would it hurt to be aware...
she never wanted or loved me... a mistake was made.......she said it was me!!!

BY: MAJESTICLADY

MY ONE TRUE LOVE

Wanna pick a fight,
Cuz its another night,
Where you tryna fuk and I'm tryna write,
Ask me to stop before I even start,
But I never put a nigguh over my art,
Why?? Cuz I never put a nigguh over my heart,
done it before and got hurt the worst,
Now its fuk em and I'ma love me first!!
Everytime love was hard,
and I was bruised and scarred,
Up went my guard,
Can't tell ya how many times I cried cause of men,
never again...
I confide in my pen,
My only fukkin friend!!
The lines on this paper hungry, so I feed em,
Words, my mind fukkin breed em,
locked behind these barz; A bitch write her way to freedom,
These lyrics like my therapy, I need em!!
remind myself of who I am when I read em!!!

BY: L4DY B

Mz. WTF You Lookin' At

(RESPECTABLE POV. TO IMMORTAL BADBOI)

What you never seen a broken woman,
one who got her own plan,
don't need a broken man,
being her crazy glue.
Not hiding shit about who I am,
you see my eyes are blue,
temperate oceans,
a circling view,
reflecting the deep of my soul's hue.
I stand firmly hand on my hip,
mouth pursed to give a headstart,
to the lip,
that anyone will get.
That's right what the fuck you lookin at,
Mz at her prime get cool with that,
cause i put myself together,
I will make me better,
my sis moody put it the best,
sayin "just a work in progress"
I took the fall for loves test,
but I can back up,
cause I'm the best,
not shielding a thing,
cause hate is like the spring,
and I got more bounce,
per ounce,
than all that,
I been held down,
a fool to a clown,
so I ask what the fuck you lookin at,
I'm a big cat,
lion in my veins,

and beast at your brains,
cause a sheep will hide its face,
when the wolf is in its place,
but don't wait for the roar,
I'm much too regal,
just give you that WTF look,
take a page from your book,
and put them in a bind,
struggle is nothing but,
one of a kind,
be a mastermind,
full frontal with that what the fuck glare,
cause what's inside me,
will never compare,
to what's out there!!!

* Was just inspired by his write. No personal shit against him. Just respected his piece and got an urge to write mine. So don't go talkin shit. Thanks Badboi for some inspiration.

BY: ARTICHOKEHEART

NIGHT FLIGHT

I rolled over and my arm touched the coolness of the space beside
me...that is when I noticed that he wasn't there... I called out over
and over again and you could even hear the fear in my voice... I was
waiting for him to answer... This wasn't fair...I looked around
wondering why would he up and leave me in the middle of the night and
not say goodbye... don't he supposed to be my guy... tears started to
fall because I was feeling this guy I can't lie... now my room is empty
and dark... it became clear that he didn't love me from the start... it
sadden me how easily I gave him my heart... how he walked out in the
middle of the night... he didn't even give his feeling one ounce of
fight... I'm crying and thinking about his night flight!!!

BY: ATLANTAMOODY

Nothing's Ever As It Seems

Nothings ever as it seems,
Stupid me for chasing dreams,
Back then you were my life,
A year together is all it took for me to know I wanted to be your wife,
However, instead I was dealt strife,
It was a slap in the face how fast we fell apart,
How fast I went from ecstasy to a broken heart,
Never seen this coming cuz things were perfect from the start,
A fairy tale love ripped at the seams,
I lost the man of my dreams!!
I Spent the next few months of my life in a depression so deep,
Every night I cried myself to sleep,
Questioned the lord..."why give me happiness if it was something i couldnt
keep??"
Took me some time to continue life without you,
Cause baby my life was all about you,
the hardest thing I've ever had to do was let you go,
But stupid me I never let it show,
I questioned myself, would he have stayed if I had let him know??
Years had passed and the questions remain,
Your memory still so alive in my brain,
Jus couldn't throw us down the drain,
I knew someday something would be able to explain,
All the unanswered questions and the pain,
Then 8 years later we were given a second chance,
Took each other's hands n made the first step to an all familiar dance,
it was as if it never ended, the 8 yrs of separation,
Seemed like just a long ass vacation,
Back into each other's arms n feelin complete,
Fallin back into a love so sweet,
Same old heart with a brand new beat,
I got him back, the man of my dreams,

THE FIRM DIVAS

But nothings ever as it seems...
you were so perfect before, not a dam thing I didn't love,
Heaven-sent, I swore you were my gift from up above,
O how time can change that,
My baby's now a strange cat,
Never use to fight,
Now its every night,
and it's not just arguin, you takin flight,
and instead of love I'm feelin fright,
this no longer feels right,
you used to treat me like a queen,
Now you're just so got dam mean,
A side of you I never seen,
O how I miss when we were thirteen
so close to showin you the door,
Cause baby I'm not happy anymore,
Head down, tears fallin on the floor,
My heart again tore,
Baby you're my best friend,
I don't wanna say goodbye again,
Don't want us to end...
We were given a second chance for a reason I'm no longer sure of,
I mean, I wanna say its love...
But lately nothings ever as it seems,
Stupid me for chasing dreams!!!

BY: L4DY B

Now I Rise

PAY NO MIND TO THE TEARS IN MY EYES.

IT'S A RELEASE.

OR IF YOU HEAR MY HEAVY SIGHS.

I'M ENJOYING PEACE.

MADE IT THROUGH THE STORMY WEATHER.

FINALLY GETTING IT TOGETHER.

GONE ARE THE SORROWFUL CRIES.

HELD ON TO FAITH-

NOW I RISE!!!

BY: LAVENDER LADY

Nursery Rhymes

To Grandma's house she goes.
The forest is thick and dark.
Scared Little Red Riding Hood picks up the pace.
Looking around her, the tree come alive.
Branches are like arms, outstretched to grab her.
Frightening noises all around her.
She starts to cry and run.
Frustrated in her little girl body, she stumbles and falls.
Closing her eyes, she makes a wish.
Transform me!
Her body trembles, screaming out, she convulses.
Clothes ripped to shreds, fall to ground.
The forest becomes silent.
The little girl is no more.
Standing, she looks down to see a grown woman's body.
Red leather boots, black leather corset, leather pants, hands with nails like talons.
Long black hair, ample breasts, but she's shocked for what she sees next.
Black wings with razor sharp tips, outstretched around her.
She giggles. Ok!
What a wish, that's not what I expected.
Starting to walk, she bends slowly to pick her basket up.
Onto Grandma's house.
She stops to smell a familiar scent, the Wolf!!!

BY: DARKANGEL68

OPEN YOUR EYES

Something you must realize...
Love don't love noone...
And life will kill you...
If you don't open your eyes.
An entitlement attitude...
Will get you nothing...
It's a sign of weakness...
being haughty & rude.
Something you must realize...
What's not earned
is worthless...
No gain in the given,
accept confusion in the loss..,
Open your eyes.
All your high expectations...
All demand,
but no appreciation...
Taking folks for granted...
Being conniving & underhanded.
Something you must realize...
You will take a fall, you will not survive...
If you don't open your eyes!!!

BY: TRANQUIL AMORE

Paper Heart

Ripping open letters,
addressed to no one I remember.
Folded promises of never,
no one loved me better.
Yours truly scribbled in no.2,
But that's all I was.
A lonely you,
and yours was never true.
I loved between sweet lines of blue,
paragraphs of tainted lies.
Melted down into pulp,
straining water out.
Salty sweet upon my pout,
a paper heart.
Folded up into a perfect square,
and tucked away.
Stained blue lines,
bleeding red.
Locked up safe inside my head!!!

BY: ARTICHOKEHEART

PLEASE HELP ME

I lay here and weep,

It's my soul I want him to keep,

please Lord help me from the heart ache that seeps,

through my heart and soul,

the one thats turning me so cold,

consumed with so much anger,

my essence is in danger at being lost but at who's cost?

just my own,

cause it's me that I own,

I can't hold unto anyones actions but mine,

and I guess it's time,

to get on my knees and beg you to please help me,

I don't wanna be weak,

but I don't wanna be the cold one who seeks,

out the wrongs in others,

because,

I'm tired and weary,

THE FIRM DIVAS

I just want to see clearly,

who's out for good,

and walk away from who's bad,

I wanna forgive him.

so that I can move on,

anger too me is worse than pain,

cause you don't have anything to gain,

sometimes I feel like I'm really going insane,

the flashbacks are so powerful,

sometimes they devour me whole,

I feel numb, and so dumb,

the hurt he infested unto my body

is nothing like the wounds he plagued on my soul,

I regress to the point of a relapse,

and this would cause mishap,

God please help me,

take this burden away!!!

BY: MS. FOXXXY

PRECIOUS

A heart of pure stone,
cemented in my chest.
Waiting for the chisel,
To carve something of interest.
Precious rock of ages,
laden with jaded sages.
It beats,
so slow beneath the sheets.
Plastering my lungs,
with the breath of songs sung.
Complacent onyx coal,
passing sludge into my soul.
Who can conquer this sorceress stone,
and put the marrow back in the bone.
Revive this ruby blood,
and drain this love of hardened mud.
Soften this sapphire gaze,
set inside mother of pearl glaze.
A heart of stone,
so precious,
yet so alone!!!

BY: ARTICHOKEHEAR

PROMICES, PROMICES

You promised to be my best ever friend to be there till the end...
You promised to be strong and true to be honest through and through...
You promised I was all you would need to be complete n whole...
You promised to be happy and true as gold...
You promised to be a man I would always respect of honor and pride...
You promised to be kind sweet and have integrity till death...
Ypu promised to allow me to be me always...
You promised to respect my choice and support my path...
You promised to help me be healthier and fit in mind body n spirit...
You promised to show me how to play and have fun n always be happy...
You promised you would never have a wondering eye...
You promised to love my children as your own...
You promised I was on a level of my own...
You promised to make me a proud wife for life...
You promised to be always there and care even if we were not together...

I honestly can say only the last promise is the one that you broke that is...
to the end of time is and will be fine in my heart soul and mind...

Good Bye it is your loss, not mine this time!!!

BY: TONICE

PUTTIN' IT DOWN

Puttin It Down
smack you around
I ain't no clown
but a woman with style
Don't get it twisted ya best get it right
cause I don't mess around...

I am that deal
and I make you get ill
with each strike that I throw
you better believe I ain't no hoe...

I'm a woman in the streetz
and a freak in the bed
I put it on you like a animal
in heat I come trill and true
so listen to what I have to say...

I am that Queen Bytch
that all hatters want to be
cause they constantly telling me what I can't do
but I'm constantly showing them
what I can do because I ain't no joke fool
and I'm PUTTIN IT DOWN!!!

BY: MAIYEN THE CHRISTIAN

READY FOR THE WORLD

Ready for the World.
Strong and Independant I am.
Stayed curled up in this corner far too long.
Struggled since the day I was born.
Grabbed the Devil by the horn.
Danced a few rounds.
As he pranced around.
Trying to gain control of my soul.
But for that I wait...
given freely to my mate.
Born a Queen searching for the right King.
Submitting my gifts to.
I Stand Proud READY FOR THE WORLD AND WHATEVER IT BRINGS
my way.
Refuse to sway from my path of discovery.
I'm Ready World...
I say Bring It On Raised 5 kids and 2 more that wasn't mine.
Gave em all a good home.
Taught em what they need to know to be Ready for the World one day.
Years of used and abused.
Never appreciated.
Shook my head as he spent his pay on crack.
Busted strung out n whack...
now he wanna come back cause he see me standing straight.
Still handlen mine.
Cause I'm a Strong Queen.
Lived in the cold mean streets and remained sweet.
World HERE I COME...
See me soar
BY: RASTALADY

Ready for the world that's always looked down on me,
Strong willed,

THE FIRM DIVAS

Never giving up,
It's my time I'm free,
Never easy,
Was me,
A scared lil girl in the corner,
So shy but always wishing she could die,
Angels always seemed to have it better than anyone,
that's what I wanted to be,
so used and abused,
blood stained tears filled my young adult years,
but im finally free,
to be who I want to be,
READY to face the world,
READY to stand proud,
never went with the crowd,
READY to face whatever comes at me,
READY TO BE THE TRUE ME
REMEMBER I AM QUEEN....
BY: MS.F0XXXY

REALITY HURTS

Reality hurts when you're sitting all alone.
Reality hurts when you have no one to call your own.
Reality hurts when you have no job or means.
Reality hurts when things are not what they seem.
Reality hurts when you're middle-aged.
Reality hurts when life turns a new page.
Reality hurts when you can't make your problems go away.
Reality hurts by the things people say.
Reality hurts when you can't pay your bills.
Reality hurts when you can't make a deal.
Reality hurts when your body is inflicted.
Reality hurts when thoughts are conflicted.
Reality hurts when no one knows who you are.
Reality hurts when an old wound leaves a scar.
Reality hurts when kids don't care like they should.
Reality hurts when you didn't but could.
Reality hurts when someone you love pass.
Reality hurts when you look into a glass.
Reality hurts when no one trust what you say.
Reality hurts when it always appear dark instead of day.
Reality hurts when you have to compete just to stay alive.
Reality hurts when it's hard to revive!!!

BY: CARAMELCAKE54

REMEMBER

Remember how we first talked,
we were like Bro' & Sis'.
Our conversations we so funny.
But then one day through a poem we did together,
you shared your true feelings to me.
I admit, it caught me by surprise.
But I can't lie I slowly was starting to feel you too.

Remember when we finally connected,
it was so wonderful,
the love between us from that point on had grew..
This was ment to be..
This we already knew.

Remember when we talked about our problem ex's,
and the bs we went through with them in the past.
Well I know the love we have will always last.

Remember when we splitted up for a temporary time,
because in our hearts there we're still,
some holes and scar tissues that needed to still heal,
and also repair our minds that was damaged from all the head trips they put
us through.

Remember when we cried to each other over the phone,
because that break up wasn't supposed to happen,
which drew us even closer.

Remember My Love!!!

BY: LAVENDER LADY

*R*HAPSODY!!!

Music..
Melody..
So sweet,
when our eyes meet.

I see my song in your soul..
With every note,
you hold..

My heart is yours, forever more.

Our rhythm..
Our rhyme..
So in tuned,
and on time.

A ballad..
Jazzy croons..

We make love a symphony,
in sensuous harmony.

Tempo..
Pitch..

Every strum and stroke on key, with expertise. We are a rhapsody.. A
melodic masterpiece!!!

BY: TRANQUIL AMOR

ROLLERCOASTER

My feeling for you is like I'm riding on a rollercoaster
Don't you see that my heart is laid out for you like a picture on a poster
If you look closely enough you could even see my heart beating
My temperature is up and I feel like I am overheating
But my mind is having me retreating
Back Into a place I don't wanna go
I have so much love to show
Yet all I am remembering is the pain
Along with all the shame
That came along with loving you
All the late night talks are gone now I don't know what to do
It was a bond that we shared
Letting me know how much you cared
Now you have me hiding and running scared
Living without you I was prepared
I felt you starting to pull away from me
Did you think I was too blind to see
Or that I was going to get down on my knees and plea
For a love that could never really be mine
I started to see that being with you was a waste of time
Yeah you have my emotions riding on a rollercoaster
But my feeling I learned to holster!!!

BY: ATLANTAMOODY

ROUND & ROUND

Round & round is where I went
Didn't you know I was heaven sent
No matter of all the trials
I will brighten up ur smile
You see I have grace and I have style
So to make you happy I will travel a thousand miles
This isn't about pussy or about dick
Or about some men or some chicks
So bring your mind back to me quick
But I know some habits is hard to kick
We all have our ups and downs
But God presence is all around
It's been lots of times I find my hands
together and knees down on the ground.
I'll never want to make my God frown
So I'm here to spread my love and joy
And to say always have faith in your heart
My journey is a never ending one
I will always find myself going around & around.
to continue to spread peace and joy!!!

BY: ATLANTAMOODY

SAND INTO GLASS

My ruby heart crushed in your hand,
finely ground into sand,
heated until each atom does expand,
and blown into the finest glass in the land.
thin and fragile marked with your brand,
envied amongst the passionate strand,
bought and sold amongst the market's stand,
made into a song by the beloved band,
while i beg to understand,
how my little glass heart can be so grand!!!

BY: ARTICHOKEHEART

SCREAM

Pretty words,
beating heart,
open wound,
pour in the salt,
dull blades tear,
rip n shred,
emotional depth of the dead,
greed expressed as honest need,
thrust the knife,
watch 'em bleed,
users the lot,
come at me with truth,
I'll discover your thinly veiled lies,
look for one to care,
don't look in my eyes,
wooden feet move thru the crowd,
wanting to SCREAM curses,
wishing to be devoured,
this blackness grows within the chest,
playing it down,
allowing self to be signaled out,
reach for stability,
in my fragility...
finding none...
I am one!!!

BY: MAJESTICLADY

SEARCH & SEIZE HER

Late at night,
down a tree lined country road,
lights flashed behind her.
She slowed to a stop.
The cop came to her window.
"Ma'am, would you step out of the car,
"She did as told.
Walking to the back of the car,
she notices the cop is close behind.
"Ma'am, put your hands on the trunk, please!"
She does as told.
His gloved hands start at her ankles and slowly move up her legs.
Closing her eyes,
waiting and wanting more,
the cop whispers in her ear.
"Ma'am,spread your legs!"
She does as told.
Hands move between her legs,
he pulls her panties down.
"Ma'am, lean forward!"
She does as told.
She feels him enter her and gasps.
Grabbing her hips and pulling her hard against him.
His flesh pounding her flesh until he is spent.
"Ma'am,you may stand up now.
"She does as told.
"Please, get into your car and drive safely!
"She does as told."
She starts the engine.
A knock on the window.
She rolls down the window.
The cop leans in and kisses her.
"Same time, tomorrow night?"
"Only if I get to be the cop!"

BY: DARKANGEL68

SEARCH & SEIZE HIM

He had a long day it work,
just at the all night store to pick up the usual.
Putting the key in the ignition, there's a knock on the window.
"Excuse me Sir,
would you step out of the car and hand me the keys. "He did as told.
"Hands on the hood, please! "He did as told.
The officer went through his pockets,
throwing the contents on the hood.
The officer had him spread his legs,
unclear of why he was being searched.
"Sir I stopped you for being incredibly hot!"
"Excuse me Ma'am, I need to get home to my wife!"
"Sir, remain quiet. "He did as told.
Her hands went up his legs, Firm touch, feeling muscles.
The hands stopped at his crotch. He breathed deep.
Her hot breath in his ear,
"Sir, remove your pants.n"He did as told.
The gloved hand began to stroke him.
He couldn't help getting aroused.
"Sir,turn around" he did as told.
The officer kneeled in front of him and took ahold of his dick.
She had it all in her mouth.
He leaned back on the hood.
His moans and growns only provoked her to suck harder.
He couldn't take much more. She was relentless.
He didn't hold back, she drank him up.
"Sir would you pull up your pants.
"He did as told.
"Please gather your belongings and get back in your car.
"He did as told.
Putting his seat belt on, there's a knock on the window...
He rolls it down. The officer leans in to kiss him.
"Next week, you be the doctor. Ok?"
"Ok, but let's do it at home."!!!

BY: DARKANGEL68

SECOND TIME AROUND

Cascading flowers
Accolades of festive praise
Attractive adorning attire
Pillars passionately positioned
gleaming smiles of satisfaction

Loved ones from afar and near
Hearts and souls joined as one
Past failures forgotten
Courageous strength starting anew
Giving and receiving gifts of love
Savoring morsels of delicacies
Dancing hand in hand to the tune of love
A foreplay of things to come
Love expressed without any inhibitions
A journey of love intertwined
A vision of me being yours and you being mine!!!

BY: CARAMELCAKE54

SECRET LOVERS

Here we are,
Meeting like this again,
Thought we were going to agree to just be friends…
You have your life and I have mine,
But I just can't get you off my mind,
I know that our love is the wrong kind,
But the love we share is real,
Can't help the way u make me feel…

Meeting at the hotel at 8,
Hoping you won't be late,
You walk in,
I'm wearing a rose in my hair
and nothing but a smile,
You begin to kiss me passionately,
And lay me across the bed,
No words were even said,
You move upon my breasts,
Sucking ever so gentle,
I know you're about to put your tongue,
To my ultimate test,
You open my thighs,
I let out a sigh,
I push ur head where my pussy calls,
The neighbors can hear my screams through the walls….

The hold you have on me,
I can't deny,
I can't let you go,
Even though you have a wife,
I need you in my life,

THE FIRM DIVAS

Secret lovers is what we are,
I gotta man,
I don't wanna let him go but,
But I don't wanna give you up…

Making love for just a while,
Deep inside my body,
Tears stream down my face,
I don't want this to ever end,
But you have your life and I have mine,
Tonight must be our final night….

Our bodies intertwined as we take our final flight,
Into ecstasy that feelz so right,
I ride you like I'm riding for dear life…
Juices flowing and nobody knowing,
This is our goodbye!!!

BY: MS.F0XXXY

SEPARATE WAYS

I was yours faithfully,
Through thick and thin,
What happened to this relationship?
Where and when?
I loved you desperately,
But I could no longer be absurd,
Had to see for real,
my vision could not be blurred,
All the lonely nights,
When you weren't around,
Looking like I was just a clown,
I will miss,
The good times,
The beautiful moments in your arms,
Making love next to the fire place,
But alas,
I can no longer think of this
I really love you but I can't be foolish,
Today I got the strength to leave you,
There's nothing left to say,
And as I wipe these tears
We must go our separate ways!!!
BY: MS.F0XXXY

I can't say that I'm surprised...
But knowing does nothing for the pain...
Residue of wishful thinking is clinging to what remains...
Reaching the proverbial fork in the road...
Fingertips lose grip of the hand that we hold...
...No longer wondering if I'm alone in this...
Conversations now confirm it's a solo trip...
Harsh words spoken from lips once kissed...

THE FIRM DIVAS

...Now form phrases of diss while pissed...

Stares poke holes in my soul from eyes I once dove in...

Your love had my nose open so wide trucks could've drove in...

Touching your skin would send shock waves to the core of me...

Oh if I only knew what the future would have in store for me;

Maybe I wouldn't have yelled so loud...

Cursed so much...

And put on such a show for the crowd...

Alas I did...And I wish this was only a phase...

I'll get my last cry in... Before we go separate ways!!!

BY: BOO ROQ NODRAMA

SEPTEMBER RAIN

September rain,
beats down on me,
has me on my knees asking God to carry me,
guide me to the place where I need to be,
take me home to where I belong,
release me from this misery,
The Rocky Mountains are no longer where I roam,
wanna be enlightened to new hights wanna go back to familiar sites,
the land of enchantment is calling me,
to the place where im free,
let the wind blow through my hair,
close my eyes and see you there,
waiting patiently,
September rain,
brings out the sunlight,
loving the feel it's so right,
makes me wanna call and take that flight,
and travel to where my heart is,
September rain,
it's time to go,
where love may await,
time to wash all those tears away!!!

BY: MS.F0XXXY

SERVED

This is for those who have been in a long relationship or marriage and it died.

Those ties that bound us together
I'm severing them.
Cutting myself free.
That leash you had around my neck, began to choke me.
I got to breathe.
Don't break my hand to hold it.
Your touch sickens me.
That thing you called love,
It's rotted and decaying.
That house isn't a home.
Vacant and empty.
The truth was just a lie.
You never loved me, how could you?
You were too busy loving yourself.
We're broke,
the kids are hungry,
how about you ask that hoe you paid to feed the kids.
Yes, I'm bitter.
Why?
Go figure.
For better,
I got worse. In sickness,
you got an STD.
For richer,
I got poor.
Till death do us part?
Fuck that,
You're severed!!!

BY: DARKANGEL68

SET FREE

Stronger mind-
Heart no longer confined…

Set free-
Of the shackles that ensnared me…

Regained my self-esteem…

Imprisoned dreams…

Set free-
Of the nightmare that hindered me.

I love again-
Gratefully..

Since I've been- Set free!!!

BY: LAVENDER LADY

SHATTERED

Used to stand so tall against the world,
now I'm feeln like a lost little girl,
I hate this life I live,
its took too much from me to forgive,

Jaded,
my give a damn, has been obliterated,

Shattered into pieces on the ground,
my strength nowhere to be found,

My eyes that once use to see so clear,
are now obstructed by a tear,

Got so much to say but actions speak louder than words,
guess I'll save that for the birds,

I'm beat,
but never been one to accept defeat,

Lately I can't seem to find my way,
feeln like what's the use in another day?

Can't do shit but pray...

To a God I'm not sure I believe in,
anything to keep you from leaving!!!

BY: L4DY B

SHE IS A TRUE DIVA

She only has two hands..
To handle so many tasks. One heart..
To spread so much love. One mind..
To make so many decisions. Two shoulders..
To carry so much weight upon.
Two feet..
To walk and balance over bumpy & slippery roads.
Her plight is not easy..
But she presses on.
Despite the scrutiny..
Her spirit remains strong. She knows humility..
Has withstanding tolerance.
Humbly, faces each challenge with refined obedience.
When she paces the floors,in the wee hours..
Her strength to endour, comes from the higher power,
that guides her through the dark..
Uplifts & heals her broken heart.
She is a survivor..
A soldier..
A fighter..
She Is A True Diva..
And noone needs to remind her of that.
She needs no pat on the back.
She's earned that name long ago..
She Is A True Diva..
And needs noone to tell her so!!!

BY: TRANQUIL AMOR

SIX FEET

I'm six feet from the edge
When I look over sometimes it
Has me thinking am I better off dead
There is nothing between me but air and the ground
How could I push these feelings down
When no one is never around
I'm tired of all the loneilness
How many time must I pass these tests
I'm doing my best
But maybe that's not good enough
Or maybe I'm not putting up enough fuss
So it always lead me back to this place and time
I can't keep saying the same old lines
How I need someone to love me
Care for me like I need to be
Emptiness is all I feel
And when that feeling takes over
I'm right back standing six feet
On the edge looking over!!!

BY: ATLANTAMOODY

SIXTEEN

Wow! 16.

It's like a lifetime away now.

I was wicked and wild then.

Wait!

I still am.

Late 1984.

Those were fun times.

Me with my hi top sneakers and parachute pants.

I was styling.

School started,

my sophmore year.

Had to go to public school,

parents couldn't afford the private boarding school.

Hated it anyhow.

Here I am in public school.

Many people didn't get where I was,

so my friends said it was reform school.

THE FIRM DIVAS

The start of my bad reputation.

I took Geometry and there he sat,

damn, he was fine.

Tall, dark tan, soft black hair, oh my.

I had to have him.

So I put the word out, who was he?

Took about a minute.

Small town. Jeff.

He had been asking about me too!!!

BY: DARKANGEL68

SPLIT PERSONALITY

Ain't been myself lately,

done let my other-self isolate me,

cause I hate me,

I know this sound crazy,

I'm just 2 gurlz tryna be 1 lady...

Constantly arguing wit myself,

silently I'm crying out for help,

this is my reality,

strugglin wit a Split Personality,

at war wit myself like ti n tip,

it's a trip!!!

BY: L4DY B

STRANGER IN MY BED

Its 2:30 where are you?/ looking through this window pane I wonder where you've been/Hoping that you're okay and that my gut isn't right/I can't sleep my mind wanders back to when/ we were once so in love till that fateful day/ the doctors said no way/ would I ever be able to have a baby/ you said you understood but I'm beginning to think/ that I am on the brink/ of losing my love, my man, my best friend/ Oh God when did his love end/It's not my fault I can't conceive/he said that in me he would believe/he should blame my uncle who took my innocence/I didn't have a defense/oh now I'm dying/A little more inside/ maybe I should just play blind/or should I leave him and never look behind/oh no he's home/ I pretend that I'm a sleep/ but deep inside I sigh/wonder if maybe I'm wrong/ if he was really working overtime/ so many thoughts race my mind are the signs sublime/ or is my imagination working overtime/Usually he reaches over and spoons me/ hmm now he's on the other side of the bed/this was what I have always dread/no I have to be strong/ I have to be wrong/I reach over to hold him/ he pushes me away/ and says "baby, I'm so tired, I need sleep"/a tear rolls from my eyes/ as I turn to my other side/ who is this "stranger in my bed"!!!

BY: MS.F0XXXY

Baby
Oh baby baby......
I so understand
we will never be able to make my seed.
One of those freak acts of nature.
Hard so hard.... Trying to be that man
Snuggled all close and tight
Trying to reassure you ...
Baby girl ...
that it's alright.
Insecurity, uninvited that Joker keep steppin in
Pulling me into this conversations mentally with me
speaking so loud to me what the hell am I gonna do
I've never desserted a mission

but Hell......momentary I ran then stop.....dead in my tracks
Throbbing deep in my heart
I still love you
Body all negative
Got you on a metal roller coast. None of this shit is intentional
but so sneaky like a bandit
negative feelings seem to just Creek right on in
Please hold on
I believe I can change
So what do you say
I Am worth the wait!!!
BY: PURE ECHO PLAY

This man I married is a stranger to me/I make him breakfast/I do all I can to please/ But he stares through me/I'm invisible/like a ghost floating through my day/I can't believe that I'm losing him./I know he's in love with HER/ I can feel it/ OMG what if my worst fears came true/What if she becomes pregnant with his baby/That's fathomless to me/ God oh God I want a baby so bad/In my soul I know that I've lost him/That all I have is me/I've lost all hope in ever trying to conceive/I feel dead inside/a shell of a woman/I wasn't good enough to love just me./He ran to her/I told him we could adopt but he so wanted a child of his own/should I finally confront him and let him know I'm wise/that our marriage is no more/That he killed me at my core/I roll myself in a ball in a corner and cry/ WHY GOD CANT I JUST DIE!!!
BY: MS.FOXXXY

STRANGER IN MY HOUSE

The house is nice and quiet.
A busy and long day.
Time for much needed sleep.
After a long hot shower,
body smooth.
Her skin is moisterized,
sweet smell of perfume.
She slips into her favorite silk gown.
The bed is calling to her.
Lights out.
She lays in the bed,
there's a noise.
It's coming from down the hall.
She tries to find a flashlight,
her phone, where did they...
He's in the room!
A hand on her mouth. "Be quiet!"
She does as told.
The other hand tosses the bedding to the floor.
He takes the strap.
of her gown and moves it off her shoulder.
His mouth is on her breast,
sucking like crazy. He says, "Stand up!" She does as told.
The gown falls to the floor.
His mouth goes to her pussy,
she grabs him by the head,
wanting more.
He says, "Lay on your back and spread your legs!"
She does as told.
His dick is hard,
he strokes and teases her,
she can't take much more.
He enters her, she goes to scream,

his hand over her mouth.
I said, be quiet!
She does as told. He pounds her hard. One leg on his shoulder.
She arches her back and matches his moves.
He gives out a growl and collapse on top of her.
Oh God honey!
You got me by surprise.
Thank God we don't have a gun!"
"Tell me,
hate to see the news,
man shot with a erection,
news at 11.!!!

BY: DARKANGEL68

STRONG WOMEN

Strong woman-

You are a survivor.

Pressin on,

despite the weight on your shoulders.

Strong woman-

Full of wisdom.

The many obstacles you've overcome.

Strong woman-

Undeniably.

Though always a lady.

For all she withstands-

She deserves the love of a strong man!!!

BY: TRANQUIL AMOR

Such Is Lyfe

Live for today..
Aspire for tomorrow...
Don' allow yourself,
to drown in sorrow.
Yesterday is past...
Can't change what is done.
Dwelling is a waste...
For time waits for no one.
Afflictions are a part of growth..
Inflictions, a part of ignorance.
Learn from both fates...
Teach from achievements and mistakes.
Such is life...
Death is inevitable.
Our next breath is not guaranteed..
So give praise for another day,
Gratefully.
Live for today...
Dream for tomorrow...
Let bygones be bygones and carry on.
Yesterday has passed...
Such is life, it's trials & tribulations..
The next moment,
can be your last!!!

BY: TRANQUIL AMOR

Surrender To Win

I surrender my will

thoughts

actions

deeds

intentions

all I am

to My Creator asking that these be ALL of His Will and pleasing to Him!
When I do this with complete abandone the Creator comes into me
completely
answering my pray and I stop fighting life on life terms and actually leads to
the true way of being a winner....
A simple prayer to start my day..........Amen!!!

BY: TONICE

TAINTED LOVE

Tainted love
I'm hip to your game
thought I would buy it
just the same...
That I was a believer
didn't think I saw you
with that beaver
should have killed you with a meat cleaver...
I saw you give her a kiss
with the sorrow
you can hit me with a miss...
Infested with God knows what
you thought you was the shit
with that strut...
Was her name Monica, or Denise
when did your loyalty cease?
Now what you get from me is peace...
Oh shit you better check your dick
heard Debbie was sick...
I knew something was wrong
why you think I long since
stopped wanting that shlong
I knew you was puting it in
places it didn't belong...
Unfaithful no longer grateful
your love is tainted
you should have just masterbated
go on get out of my life
go find yourself a new wife!!!

BY: MS.FOXXXY

THE DAY I WALKED OUT

The day I walked out was a liberating day for me.
The day I walked out, I knew it was time to be free.
The day I walked out, I had, had enough.
The day I walked out I knew things would be tough.
The day I walked out I only had a few things of my own.
The day I walked out of a marriage that was blown.
The day I walked out emotionally I started to heal.
The day I walked out no more secrets or lies to reveal.
The day I walked out with no money in my pocket.
The day I walked out family sent money like a rocket.
The day I walked out the pain on my son's face...it's hard to erase.
The day I walked out, things that were said to paint me a disgrace.
The day I walked out, I went against the norm.
The day I walked out drenched in mental storms.
The day I walked out, glad I did it while still alive.
The day I walked out, I knew I would survive.
The day I walked out I knew I deserved better if only it came from me.
The day I walked out I was embraced by my dignity!!!

BY: CARAMELCAKE54

THE PAIN

The Pain is way too deep and way too much for me to bare

I see myself falling in despair and letting go of the rope

I don't see no hope or nothing

all I see is a deep black hole

I am stuck and lost and no one can find me

to be or not to be is the question they ask me but I have no answer

nothing to answer to nothing to lean on so what am I to do.

I don't know what to do or where to turn to

I am just so confused at this time.

The Pain of a broken soul is not good to have but hey what can I say?

what can I expect?

And why can't I give my heart to the sky does that make sense?

Well if it don't F' it

then I am just being me

and if they don't like me screw them and screw what they talking about

real talk cause all I feel is... THE PAIN!!!

BY: MAIYEN THE CHRISTIAN

THE SAME GUY

CHORUS:
I can't believe me and my sis'
Been talking to the same guy,
The same guy,
He's the man of each of our dreamz,
WE both love the same guy or so it seems,
I thought he was someone I could trust,
But hes been doubling up with both of us,
Let's get together and make the bust,
Wait till he sees us Divas both together,
Doesn't he know we are sisters and can make it through any weather!!!

No need to ask why / did I have to lie / once... twice... fly / they both love The Same Guy
Oh wow / who am I / the brotha with the gift of gab / the walk / the talk / the all New York swag
Plus I know how to add / subtract and measure / one plus one is double fun / twice as better
Double the pleasure / like the gum in your mouth / single try'na mingle / while I'm finding a spouse!!!
BY: POETICAL WORD PLAY

Hey Artichoke,
I want to introduce you to this guy,
I've been seeing,
Oh my, he's the man of my dreams,
His body makes me scream,
A light skinned brotha,
He makes me feel loved,
And makes my pussy cream,
we made love all thru the night!!!
BY: MS.F0XXXY

THE FIRM DIVAS

Oh Foxxxy,
you met someone,
I did too,
got my skin callin,
for him to come through,
writing me love songs,
whispering in my ear,
all the things I long,
to hear,
from hopes and dreams,
to gettin in my jeans,
eyes that stare right through me,
lips that don't miss,
girl I better quit,
before I make you want to see,
how you can get his kiss!!!

BY: ARTICHOKEHEART

So along came Heart this Sexy Awesome Diva / checked the clothes and the cologne / then I set out to meet her

Think'n Peter & the Beaver / fuck'n / let's make it happen / dropped a line or two / of Brooklyn style rap'n

Now we midnight cap'n / knock'n boots and stuff / her little thug / wants the plug / so rough and tough

So I hit her in the socket / without come'n out my pocket / but still gave a little love / with Brooklyn pic in the locket...

Not will'n to stop it / met Diva number two / step to her like (((DAMN FOX))) what up what it do

She didn't have a clue / about the other Ms. Lady / so I sent out the Word Play / to one day rock her baby

She started out with a maybe / then lunch and dinner / I switched gears to Poetical / know'n that would win her

Like... Damn you see that / Lord... what the heck / she said "what" / I see donkey / without the Shreck

Titties in check / may I rest on your pillow / can I rub my ding dong / against your pussy willow!!!

BY: POETICAL WORD PLAY

THE FIRM DIVAS

My man is so sweet,
he picked me up last night for a dinner and a treat..
you should have seen that ride,
a Mercedes,
he was looking so tight!!!
BY: MS.F0XXXY:

Girl you gonna laugh,
but mine does too,
told me in class,
is what he is born to do,
though in that car,
we didn't get far,
before I was doin unclassy things,
so I take it this is your earring,
I have a similar pair,
so before I went to trippin,
I thought I'd compare,
but my mind wasn't slippin,
this is all becoming clear!!!
BY: ARTICHOKEHEART

Really that's weird... hmm, what does your man do for a living...
Mine's name is Mike,
but I call him Brooklyn...
OMG, don't tell me that's your guy's name....
oh no we can't be in love with The Same Guy....
mine's light skinned with gorgeous eyes...
got a body that makes me wanna die...
don't tell me that's your guy!!!
BY: MS.F0XXXY

Girl you gonna think this is crazy,
mine goes by Brooklyn but I call him baby,
he tryin to make it in the rap game,
met him at a show,
and never been the same,
up to this point,

no reason to complain,
I find it hard to believe,
two men have that name!!!
BY: ARTICHOKEHEART

         Oh yeah we need to set a trap...
         catch this fool in his own rap...
         who does he think he is he's just a man and were kin...
         we both can't be with the same guy!!!
         BY: MS.F0XXXY:

We caught this dude in a lie,
he must not know you my twin,
how bold to think he could get by,
and that you and I,
wouldnt get to talkin,
but I have a plan,
to show this man,
just who he fuckin,
dodgin and duckin,
I was seeing him tonight,
I'll tell him I have a treat,
wanna do him right,
two girls can't be beat,
but what a sight,
when you and I take a seat!!!
BY: ARTICHOKEHEART

THE FIRM DIVAS

I was in it for the thrill so / along came spider / hehehe / I crept up and slept up right beside her

Mixed up the cider / with a little bit of tonic / added the vodka / knocked and rocked her

I was in come'n out / like an adultery spouse / big bad wolf / on my way to Heart's house

No moral... No story / a nigga just got it good / swag so official / and I'm so damn hood

Niggas just wish they could / get one of these Divas / but I bottled 'em up / and got two of them liters...

Then came the day / when hell came my way / with nothing to say / just hell to pay

I just wanted to play / but now I'm cashed out / ass out / two DIVAGIRLS like / "yo... what's that about"

Jaw dropped / lip hang'n / no words claim'n / the things I was doin / the two I was screw'n

Now I'm boo~hoo'n / in the midst of my lame lie / how can I explain / different love but THE SAME GUY!!!

BY: POETICAL WORD PLAY

THE SMILE IN MY VOICE

Now I have a smile in my voice

no longer broken because of the form of pain and dropping tears.

I have a smile in my voice...

No more misery or anger...

The old tune my voice had carried.

People here can hear the joy and smile in my voice now-a-days,

compared to yesterday's emotions that was within me.

I have a smile in my voice...

Why do I now have a smile in my voice because I've let go,

and let God take control.

And my new man, who has my heart in a positive and strong state of

mind.

I love you Bae... Thank you for being there and loving me!!!

BY: LAVENDER LADY

THE STORM SHALL PASS

Struggles & strife-

that's life.

Nothin comes easy,

Believe me.

Face your fears, and don't break.

Shed your tears,

bare the heartache.

Never stop hopin-

When one door closes,

another one opens.

It's just a test,

not meant to last.

So press on-

the storm shall pass!!!

BY: TRANQUIL AMOR

THE SUN IS HERE

The sun is hear,

after the stormy rain,

and rough waves we overcame.

I'm back to the old me

I left the state of misery,

and never to return.

The sun is out I found my love,

no need to search anymore,

because me,

he adores as the roses gloom so beautifully

my feelings is feeling the vibe of sunshine and energy.

The sun is out now it's time for to shine!!!

BY: LAVENDER LADY

THE TIME HAS ARRIVED

The time has arrived...
To move on with my life.
There's nothing left here to do...
I've exhausted every avenue.
Deep in my heart, I know... I must go...
On to the next plateau.
The time has arrived...
To spread my wings and fly.
So I shall soar...
Over the new horizon, awaits so much more.
Reaching higher...
Following my heart's desire...
My need has become dire.
To cut loose the ties that bind me...
Leaving the said and done behind me.
The time has arrived...
To apply all acheived from my toil and strive...
And rise.
Up and above the mountain peaks...
For what I soul yen, I shall seek.
New goals, I aim to reach.
This part of my life has reached its drought...
Now I thirst...
The time has arrived, for me to branch out!!!

BY: TRANQUIL AMOR

THE TRAVELING PANTS

These pants like family have been through hell, from every fight to nights in jail, in despair the knees have been worn, they hug my butt to tease the men, my sisters know how this is true, too tight, too short out of date doesn't matter in the least, they tend to fit every mood, hearts n pants make no sense yet for us they do, passed around, beaten, thrown out only to be retrieved, patched as they can be, hanging by a thread at times, strength felt but unseen, they forgive those extra inches as family forgives trespasses, hell they'll even lie for me, show me as tight and firm at 39 as I was at 20... yeah I love these pants...woven through days of blue, seen their share of red, never once gave me cause to regret investing myself in family and pants!!!   *BY: MAJESTICLADY*

These pants have seen us through thick and thin and taking us places where we have been. They fit firm on all of us Divas that much is true and you girls knows just how much I love you. Those pants or more than pants they are like our best friends and they have seen us through every trend. We Divas wear those pants well and when we are together we will never fell. Those pants will take us to then end of time and they will help us out of any bind!!!   *BY: ATLANTAMOODY*

These pants not anyone could fit,
hips to shoes,
they just don't quit,
accentuating the way we walk,
putting the sway in swagger,
more confidence in the talk,
just from some travelling pants,
there's a kind for every mood,
boot cut or flared,
skinny when we are feeling good,
hugging a diva just right,
leaving some thinking,

they wish they could hold that tight,
light fade or dark denim
jeans just look better,
with a diva travelling in em,
like these pants we come in all sizes,
colors and shapes,
but no surprises,
come together as one,
but just like travelling pants,
One day will be gone!!!
BY: ARTICHOKEHEART

These traveling pants I wear have seen some things. From salvation to a wedding ring. These pants have been worn through the trials and test of life. Even when no longer a wife. These pants have bent and hit every curve. Through anxiety and feelings that disturb. This pants appear to be magical, they continue to fit as I grow. Even when I sit down, my panties from above may show. Wearing these pants against the elements of the world. Through many ups and down. I have learned to be a big girl. For some have tried to remove my pants to get what's underneath. Believing in the Lord is what my soul seek. These traveling pants has been around for a very long time. These traveling pants are exclusively mine!!!   *BY: CARAMELCAKE*

Traveling Pants
May go drifting
From time-to-time
Yet, staying True
Always . In return
Thru the harshest of
Winds, the slashing
Unable to keep
them away.. Even in
Burst against
Mountains of thrashing
Tribulations.
Situations

Will not fade them Away.
Embarking amongst the
Trunks of tallest troubles They lead us to
Shaded Protection
Never thinking
Over.. Would be in
Reaching or Racing
To the top.
Still keeps the Humor in Letting the final
Drop --- to the
Many feet
No defeat ,,, Just
Leveling down
Keeping Hearts in
Motion.
Where Life
Can become a
Commotion
Even thru the
Unfastened loose-ends
They are
Our Family Our Friends . Our STRENGTH!!!
BY: PURPLE3RAIN.MARIA

Pants dat give me full support; keep my curves lookin so fuckin amazin. What I love most is how reliable they are. They are just like my sisters never failin. When I was so far down in da valley, though I had no1 to turn to, my sisters came lifted me up, prayed me through my darkest tymes. Da pants saturated in my blood, contantly catchin my black tears. Some days I wonder how will I make it, what am I goin to wear then both come to my rescue. My sisters we have a unbreakable bond, sure we have been through hell, lames try to come between us but just as da pants they hold up through tragedy, heartache, misery, torture, sufferin, da pourin rain, but when it's all said and done we stand in love, joy, peace, hope, an happiness. Just as da sky is never endin, neither is our Sisterhood Bond. God, I have to come an say thank you, not for your grace & mercy you have shown and gave me tyme after tyme, or how you loved me even through my own selfishfaults, an my disappointments in Your eyes. I come now to thank you for placing these beautiful amazin women in my lyfe who I am blessed to call not only my friends but my Sisters. I lift them up to you now God, to heal, restore, and give them strength. Shower them wit love an joy. I pray you keep them and their family, allow your angels to guide and watch over them day an nyte. Order their steps, an bless them in every way, open up doors in their lives dat noone can close. Dry their tears. Keep them save God, let them know how much I love them an appreciate them. Never let their voices be silenced. Thank you God for da strong women you placed in my lyfe. Amen!!!

BY: KINKYPRINCESS

These pants I've worn,
through many storms..
They've held up,
through the slosh and mud..
They've been slightly tattered..
Spilt on, and splattered..
Yet, no matter the weather~
They hold together..
To wear another day..
Without becoming frayed..
Just like a reliable friend~
We've been through thick and thin.
These pants are durable and strong..
Like the love I have for my sisterhood~
An unbreakable bond.
Through every season change~
The close knit remains the same..
Never loosening at the seams..
Pockets full of memories..
Like a true friendship's endurance~
These pants mean alot to me!!!
BY: TRANQUIL AMOR

I look at these pants all tattered and torn/wondering when last they were worn/my sister had them sent/when she heard me vent/told me to wear them with pride/so The Sisterhood never died/they look like a size five/how am I...gonna get all this thyckness in?/I called her up buggin/she said calm down /those pants have a magic all their own/they fit whoever needs em to/here's what you do/just wet em and hang em to dry/the next time you feel the need to cry/they will fit/then just sit/back and relax/you will feel /the whole sisterhood envelop you/I swear its real/now here's the deal/when you feel you are able to pass them along/give them to A Sister who is really down/these pants have travelled many miles/through many towns/seen many smiles and many frowns/dealt with the used and abused/as they are passed along/helping those who have been wronged/you may wonder how this could be/a simple pair of pants..you see/is so much more/they do their part/because they are a gift from the heart/passed down the line/SISTER to SISTER!!!

BY: RASTALADY

They been poked at
and spoke on
sold to the wrong group
left out and confused
but through it all we stuck it out
haters came and haters go
through it all
we fought the good battle
we let them know that we are not no old torn pants
that they can just use and run over
they fight one
they got to fight all
and we are like the million pants march
so mess with use and you will die
and that ain't lie,
because I love my Sisters
and try me and see
I can show you better than tell you!!!
BY: MAIYEN THE CHRISTIAN

Mother ,lover, teacher, worker,
a woman's work is never done...
chauffeur, chef, maid, butler and oh so many countless others,

to many jobs to list one by one...
and only another woman can truly know how it feels to be one...
this is the tie that binds, and can never be undone...
wisely woven, with sturdy stitches,
sisterhoods fabric is tougher than Teflon...
with true bonds of friendship and solidarity...
to find sum1 who simply "gets you" is a rarity...
the perfect fit, like comfortable jeans
tailor made to accentuate my best qualities...
even when we don't agree,
my sisters always there to comfort
and bring out the best in me...
we may come from different walks of life,
but we travel the same roads...
as my sisters keeper, I'll gladly share her load..
knowing there will come a time when mine will get heavy...!!!
it's nice to know my sister will in return be there for me
BY: GUDGIRLGONEBAD601

My traveling pants fit me well
Been through Hell
And back, here we go again
Rain and wind have broken them in
Just like a good ole friend
Worn and stained but I wear them
Til they go thin
It's not that they look the best
But these pants have been through
The test of time
Much like my friends
The traveling pants go with me
Everywhere and anywhere
Good times and bad times
They're always the perfect fit
I'll send them on to the next woman
As my gift

THE FIRM DIVAS

To the young who sometimes
Wonder who is a friend!!!
BY: DARKANGEL68

The traveling pants
I wear mine kinda baggy
but comfortable
there a little worn
and frayed but still mine
I don't wanna ever get rid of them
they are my favorite and feel good wearing them
there like how I feel with my friends
I don't want to get rid of them
I wanna keep them close
there a little goofy
and worn but there mine
they have been through hell
and back with me
just like my pants.
even if I don't have a daughter of my own
I will pass my pants on to my step-daughter
and listen to the stories she will tell!!!
BY: SQUIRREL86

They are just a symbol of the times.
Bell-bottoms or hip huggers may have been there.
However, as we grow we have to mend the rips and tears of rugged wear.
The patches of peace and little mushrooms hide the holes of time.
The adjustments made to fit are like the changing of one's mind.
The gaining weight or gaining height
is a time to change the pants to a well-adjusted skirt.
Give the sides a slice of color polyester
or a patch of quilting ends to stretch
the waist to fit and put on some lace to add length to the hem!
Again, changing the look but keeping the style
and comfort of a well-cared for friend
that is closer than the one

THE FIRM DIVAS

is bought in the high priced boutiques of the fashion mall!
A sister is not always the one
you had growing up with but the relationship
is made for an everlasting journey of care and love!
Forgiving me my weakness for sweet treats
and me forgiving the lack of boutique fashions!
Together forever bonded by familiarities'
and unconditional trust.
A sisterhood mended by love!!!
BY: TONICE

Through many trials
and tribulations I wear these pants
They've been broken in, soaked through
Tattered and bruised
But what's kept them worn
Is through any weather
They have been dependable
Like a sister
We laugh
We fight
We cry
We hold each other tight
These pants dear sister
Have seen war
The one that rages from within
The wars that happen between friends
The Wars brought upon from men
Sometimes we grow out of them
And they get lost
But we love them still
at any cost
Sometimes you have to let them go
so that they can flourish and grow
But never give up on them
Why?
Because each both the sisters and the pants

THE FIRM DIVAS

Come into your life for a reason
Bell bottoms as child I wore in the autumn
School Chums playing tag
Those skinny jeans while you're a teen
Friends helping you become homecoming queen
Maternity pants spell life
My matron of honor when I became his wife
Our Style and our pants change through the years
Our friends see us thru the tears
They are alike
They are comfortable
And together fit just right
They are there for you to guide you to the light
They go through different stages
Rages and engagements
But pants like sisters
May get old And full of holes
Fights may have made us part
BUT TRUE SISTERS WILL FORGIVE
Because we have all worn the same pants
we're traveling in!!!
BY: MS.F0XXXY

These old pants are worn,
Faded, tattered, n torn...
But it was in them the woman in me was born,
They were once too big, then once to tight,
Now they fit just right,
Hug me where it's needed,
Provide comfort where im seated,
Been ripped by the walls I've had to climb,
covered my ass time after time,
Thru my hardest fights,
To the coldest nights...
These pants have become my own,
They've been sown,
Together weve grown...

THE FIRM DIVAS

Thru all the shit,
We now a perfect fit!!!
BY: L4DY B

THE TROUBLE WITH LOVE

The trouble with love is,
it takes you to the highest mountaintop
then drops you like a rock.
It's the best drug,
the biggest high that you can't come down from,
then suddenly the needle gets jerked out and your left fiending.
The trouble with love is,
when you're in it, you brag,
you boast about how that person is the most,
the greatest,
then you hurry to erase their name from your memory when it's over. The
trouble with love is,
you can never have enough,
it's the craving you can't fill,
it hurts till you can't breathe,
and you want more, and more.
The trouble with love is,
every damn song you hear makes sense,
love or hate it,
you sing along,
cursing at the radio.
The trouble with love is,
I want it, got to have it,
I will go to extremes to keep it,
rejoice that I have it,
and yell at the Devil if I don't!!!

BY: DARKANGEL68

THESE EYES *PAIN & GLORY*

These eyes have seen life come and go.
These eyes,
have held joy and sorrow.
As I reflect on years gone by..
And look forward, with hope,
to another tomorrow.
These eyes have been a silent witness.
These eyes, have cried behind cruel injustice.
When there was nothing I could do..
Feeling so damn helpless.
These eyes are filled with apassionate fire.
These eyes are the portal to my deepest desires.
As I trudge forward in my journey for peace..
My body grows weary, but my spirit never tires.
These eyes have seen visions of what is yet to come.
These eyes have seen many moons and suns.
Through many trials, I've acquired much knowledge and wisdom.
These eyes, tell my history.
These eyes can reveal every testimony.
Just look into them and you'll see..
Pain and Glory!!!

BY: TRANQUIL AMOR

Through Time

Throughout time, you've been here.
In the Garden of Eden you whispered to Eve, cursing all women for eternity.
Through century after century you have convinced women of every race and color.
You've filled their heads with delusions of grandeur.
Many times you have been caught only to be villified by a lesser woman.
You hide in the open, waiting for your prey.
Jumping at the chance to find a woman, hurt, scared and alone.
Your looks don't make you stand out that much but you make up for it with your charm.
You're not rich but you'll make due.
Educated but no genius.
A real man depises you.
After you plant your seed of lies, if that woman tells those lies to another man, he knows.
You're quick to step in, degrading all men that call you on your game.
I've seen you many times in my life.
You may not recognize me now, I'm a grown woman.
You slithered around me as a child, tempted me as a teenager, and as a Mother.
The woman I am now,smells you a mile away.
Promises of a life I've been denied.
You tried to convince me that yours is the greatest love I'll know.
Making love to me for hours and days, pleasing me in every way you know how,
but I stopped you dead in your tracks.
I asked the questions nobody would ask.
Why? How? Your anger told me everything!!!

BY: DARKANGEL68

Under His Spell

I come to you my dear with a worried mind.
Something has taken ahold of me and I'm losing control.
It's not something I can easily describe.
He came to me when I didn't expect it.
Whispered words of passion.
My heart raced, my body on fire.
This is not normal for me.
I gave you my promise of love.
Alas I cannot deny this craving for him,
this deep desire for his touch.
I have not given in to the temptations of the flesh.
Maybe it's the spell I'm under or is he the Devil himself.
Help me Dear!
I'm under his spell!!!
BY: DARKANGEL68

This man that you talk of,
he's making you think sinful things.
We both took our vows and we both wear the rings.
Is he really as good as I am?
You tell me this truth as I am still your man.
Can he provide the same love that I give,
could he go through what we both do and then turn and forgive.
I feel that he is the Devil himself,
is it his whispered lies or his slick talkin wealth.
I may not be the most amazing man,
but I love like no other man can.
I will always protect you, and make you feel safe,
needed and loved and to give and not take.

So please my sweet darling,
in true honesty,
please don't feel tempted,
please lay down with me.
Hold me,
and feel all the love that I give and let's stay together,
and in happiness live.
You can beat temptation,
were perfect you see.
No other couple could remain so happy.
Give me the chance to prove to your soul,
that men such as that haven't got a good loving soul.
He tried to tempt my angel but she will see the light,
cause I know that she always will choose the path that is right!!!
BY: T.B.T

*U*NIFIED *C*ONTRADICTION

Loaded with meaning so meaningless, full of empty emotion, barren fields of thought covered in moss, heart pounding in a dead chest, dreams of freedom, already free, music floating silently, nightmares before wakened eyes, truth full of lies, darkness shining bright as the sun, moon and stars above none to see, contradiction unified in agreement, delusional reality, imagination is the key to an unlocked door, empty room filled with faces, featureless observers on the floor, clearly defined contours, I say im done, you give me more, perfect imperfection!!!

BY: MAJESTICLADY

United We Are...

(THE FIRM DIVAS)

ORIGIN OF A DIVA:
Italian, literally, goddess, from Latin, feminine of divus divine, god —
more at DEITY
First Known Use: 1883
A Diva is a celebrated female singer.
The term is used to describe a woman of outstanding talent in the world
of opera,
and, by extension, in theatre, cinema and popular music.and for us in
the world of poetry...

A Sisterhood:
An association of women, or things which are considered to be feminine.
1. The state or relationship of being a sister or sisters.
2. The quality of being sisterly.
3. A society, especially a religious society, of women.
4. Association or unification of women in a common cause.

These women of all ages, nationalities, and origin, have come together,
WHY?
FOR THE LOVE OF THEIR CRAFT AND THE COMMON BOND
THAT THROUGH POETRY THIER VOICES CAN BE HEARD!!!

Divas... The name of The Fam',
ain't in it for the fame or the glam,
My Sistas and I joined together in unity,
contributing to the Blog Community,
ain't here for the fighting,
let me enlisting you with these words that I'm writin,
not afraid,
we artist like Kincaid,
but some of yall act like you getting paid,

how dare you try to invade,
the walls of this home that we made,
every poem like a brick that we've laid,
you can try to take us down if you think you could,
we've put in work as a Family, A Sisterhood if you would,
Together we stand tall, divided we fall"
that pretty much say it all!!!
BY: L4D Y B

There may be a lot us,
but together we are one as a family.
I love my Diva Sistas...
They're like big sisters I've never had.
We're bigger and better,
so fuck them hater's...
In my book, I call them LOW-RATERS.
Why because I'll alway's have love for my DIVA SISTAS!!!
BY: LAVENDER LADY

A goddess is a female deity.
In some cultures goddesses are associated with Earth, motherhood, love, and the household.
In other cultures, goddesses also rules over war, death, and destruction as well as healing.

Una diosa es una deidad femenina.
En algunas culturas diosas están asociados con la tierra, la maternidad, el amor y la familia.
En otras culturas, diosas también gobernar guerra, muerte, destrucción así como curación.

sisterhood - an association or society of women who are linked together by a common religion or trade or interest sistership

association - a formal organization of people or groups of people; "he joined the Modern Language Association"

THE FIRM DIVAS

Sisterhood - une association ou une société de femmes qui sont liés par une religion commune ou de commerce ou des intérêts sistership

Association - une organisation formelle des personnes ou groupes de personnes ; "Il a rejoint l'Association de langue moderne"

IN ANY LANGUAGE IT MEANS THE SAME!!!!
EVERY WOMAN IS A GODDESS
WE ARE HERE TO EMBRACE IT AND SUPPORT EACH OTHER
THIS STARTED OUT AS A DREAM AND HAS BECOME REALITY...

LIKE US OR NOT WE ARE NOT GOING ANYWHERE AND WE WILL
NOT BACK DOWN,
THE LOVE THAT I HAVE FOR MY SISTERS IS EQUAL TO THE
LOVE I HAVE FOR MY BLOOD SISTER...
MESS WITH ONE YOU WILL DEAL WITH US ALL....

WE CRAVE PEACE AND LOVE AND OUR MISSION IS CLEAR,
BY: MS.F0XXXY

We come together as one and we make it do wat it.
We are in this together and we take no drama from noone
we don't play the mind games or try and hate on what the outsiders do
because we are to good for that.
We are as one and that makes us UNITY
and we gonna stick it through
no matter who decides to leave the crew we will still be at the top and not at
the bottom.
So think before you mess with one of us because you mess with one you
messing with all
we will jump on you like a tick sucking on your blood
cuz we are The Firm Divas and we do it BIG!

So don't hate just know that we stick together through hot or cold
and we make it through the storm
Because we are UNITY and that is what we are all about...

THE FIRM DIVAS

A Little Note:
For all the Hatters, Backstabbers, Or outsiders that don't like us or think we are trouble.
Dear we are not trouble you are and you're messing with the wrong people so like I said before don't step up like you're hard!!!
BY: MAIYEN THE CHRISTIAN

My motto is, UNITED WE STAND, DIVIDED WE FALL.
Rather fitting for THE FIRM DIVAS.
Funny, when you go against a group of women
we grow stronger, together.
A common thread has been woven between us.
Through lifes hard times, we persevier.
We can take a hit and just dust ourselves off, jumping up swinging.
You may say I'm down but don't count me out.
A whisper, a few idle words, inuendoes, try again.
I strug them off.
Throw me to the wolves, that's cool, I'll tame the savage beast
Man or woman, I'll take you on.
Fear is not an option.
Stand up, make yourself known.
Dont hide.
Maybe you're afraid I'll meet you eye to eye, toe to toe.
Beware I do not come alone.
Always A DIVA to take up a cause.
Standing united, hand in hand!!!
BY: DARKANGEL68

We band together..
Hand in hand together.
Ink & pen together..
We stand together.
I have loyalty,
to my sisterhood.
Diva's unity,
draws envy.
It's all good.

THE FIRM DIVAS

Though always A Lady
Let it not be misunderstood...
Our strength will always supersede, the enemy.
Haters love to hate us.
Try to cause chaos.
Their M.O.,
is to separate us.
To no prevail
You can't fade us.
We are survivors..
Not nose divers.
We are strivers..
Even hard core writers (riders).
We are Family..
A strong entity.
What was once a dream,
has become a reality.
No one can take that away.
The Divas are here to stay.
Sorry to burst bubbles
When tomorrow comes,
and we're not gone. (lol)
We keep pressing on.
No, this ain't no game..
Check the name - Tranquil Amor.
Peace to the haters.
Much love to my Sisters.
BY: TRANQUIL AMOR

THE FIRM DIVAS

We stand forever together
More than two birds are a feather
When are we gonna stop
Never!
Our words are meant to be heard
We will put your emotions on overload
Nothing but the best come from us
Even through all the old drama and chaos
The Divas walk tall every day
Always remember we are here to stay
You don't have believe a word I say
Because ours words gonna jump off the pages and slap you
Then you will see we are the best and it isn't a damn thing you can do
The Divas stand proud and tall
Here to take on any of y'all
A come one come all
Then The Divas will show you how it's done!!!

BY: ATLANTAMOODY

Sisterhood:
A gathering of woman,
coming as one,
sharing a love of family,
through poetry,
stories of rhymes,
laughs and hard times,
with a grand plan,
of giving all a chance,
to shine...

Diva:
Not just an attitude,
a way of life,
coming up from darkness,
being a lady through strife,
judge for yourself,

THE FIRM DIVAS

who can claim this name,
but safely say we are not all the same,
we each shine in a different light
Diva Sisterhood:
now together huddled in a small group,
women of a firm revolution,
a poetic troop,
equal desire,
equal drive,
equal power to survive,
with style and grace,
no prima donna fits,
just pens in hands,
and ink that never quits!!!
BY: ARTICHOKEHEART

We are THE FIRM DIVAS AND WE WILL PERSAVERE!!!!!!

Nous sommes LA FIRME DIVAS et nous sera PERSAVERE !!!!!

είμαστε η ΕΠΙΧΕΊΡΗΣΗ DIVAS και ΕΜΕΊΣ θα PERSAVERE!!!!!

我们是公司舞蹈天后，我们将 PERSAVERE!!!!!!!

Somos la empresa DIVAS Y que será PERSAVERE

**WE ARE THE WOMEN OF POETRY....
WE ARE THE FIRM DIVAS!!!!!!**

UNITED WE STAND

Together united in which we stand
I'm your woman and you're my man
I can feel the love flowing between us
As we walk hand in hand
On the path to happiness is what we took
We didn't walk it together on no we ran
Looking in your eyes on our special day
While we put on each other bands
Saying it to the world once again
That I'm your woman and you're my man
Stand proud and tall cause forever
We will know united in which we'll stand
Now that day is over and gone
Our love will stay blessed and strong
Living life as it should be
Our love shining brightly so the whole world can see
Just how much you mean to me
They will see how you stand up
and do what a man supposed to do
Because our vows tied us together
so you will do what you need to do
United we stand
will be a beginning to our end
Living as husband and wife and no longer in sin!!!

BY: ATLANTAMOODY

WAITING TO EXHALE

Breathe in,
Release,
Need to calm my nerves,
I can't think,
Jumbled thoughts,
Trace my mind,
Don't wanna leave anything behind,
But my time has almost run out,
My words no longer need to be heard,
My voice is hoarse,
Has this run its course,
The sands have reached an impasse,
I guess it can't always last,
The hour glass is half past,
Shattered dreams,
Are all I see,
Nothing left to believe,
I take a deep breath,
And wait to exhale,
Is this truth or just a fable,
No label,
Of who I am,
I am me,
That's who I am,
I can't be you,
Just like you can't be me,
I lie in wait,
And see where fate,
Takes me,
I take a deep breath,
And exhale
I just hope where I go I no longer fail!!!

BY: MS.F0XXXY

WAVES OF TURMOIL

An agonizing cry coupled with a tumultuous frame of mind
Watered streams released with a gentle flow of memories left behind
Reasoning rationalized in a formidable way
The taciturnity of emotions kept at the bay of daring things not to say
The tutelage of defense relating to the contractions of the heart
Mental wars raging that's intellectually hard to outwit or outsmart
Ubiquitous fecal matter flying to the corners of the globe
Many prominent figures asking to be disrobed
The changing of the guards passing to the next generation
Unresolved issues magnified with greater proliferation
helpless harnesses worn around the throat
Arrested development stunted choke
Gesticulating in the movement of life as the wind blow
Some rich, some destitute without knowing where to go
Gregariously mingling in the gigantic room of the world
In the end solitude will embrace every man, woman, boy and girl!!!

BY: CARAMELCAKE54

WE ARE STILL DIVAS

Lightning and thunder..
A world asunder..

Only a few still alive..

No doubt,
only the strong survive..

The weak have perished..

Your memory,
shall be cherished..

The strong-willed,
has healed..
Time to rebuild.
A new foundation..

A new nation..
Never mind the nonsense..

For the sake of peace,
I welcome the silence..

If all we have for now,
is just us- Then blessed is our unity..

We are still, The Divas.
One pen, One love..

We shall always rise above!!!

BY: TRANQUIL AMOR

WHY

Why...
Disappeared was the love I felt for you
In its place is all the hateful things to that you do
The evil eye that you seem to give me
Now I'm praying for you to just set me free
Late at night would be so easy for me to flee
But I was never someone that was known to run
I tried hard to work things out believe me that ain't fun
I have wake up and pointing in my face is your gun
Why...
when you suppose to love me
And treat me like a woman supposed to be
I'm not a hard person to love
You use to say I was sent from heaven above
To bring you joy and happiness
I remember how you used to sleep soundly on my breast
But now our home isn't even allowed any guest
And At night I can't get any rest
Why...
I'm too afraid to show people what you put me thru
People see the pain in my eyes from the blood that you drew
You wasn't like this in the beginning
Now I hear you talking about me with you friends and grinning
Would I ever have and that happy ending
Why...
Please tell me why I stay
For you to continue to hurt me day after day
I can't tell anyone I'm afraid of them judging me
And more afraid of what they will say to me
Living this life isn't easy you see

THE FIRM DIVAS

Why…
The time when I would pack my begs
The first night you go to sleep without holding yourself over my legs
I know you feel the time is ending for us
Believe as soon as it's possible I'm jumping on the nearest bus
Then you would be stuck asking yourself
Why!!!

BY: ATLANTAMOODY

WE'VE COME SO FAR

You watched me suffer my consequence
Not using my common senses.

Made many mistakes,
that caused me heartaches.

As you were growin,
I was growin too...
So young when I had you.

It was hell, but I learned my lessons well.

Though it was hard,
We've come so far!!!
BY: TRANQUIL AMOR

When I seen her overcome,

I became a believer,
that it can be done.

When I made mistakes,
she soothed the heartaches.

People we know,
say we became tough as nails...
Hard knock lessons is how we prevailed.

Tho it was hard,
We've come so far!!!
BY: LAVENDER LADY

WHEN A WOMAN LOVES

When a woman loves it's for real...
she digz down deep to let you know just how she feels...
She needz to feel wanted...
she wants to see that u think she's beautiful and flaunted...
When a woman loves it's for life...
through good and bad times...
she'll become your wife...
through sickness and health...
for richer or poorer...
she shows you she's always in your corner...
When a woman loves it comes from the depths of her soul...
her loyalty is a site to behold...
she eternally will be yours...
she brings it from her core...
When a woman loves it's beautiful...
candlelight and bubble bathes...
she wants to show you her love will last...
the hands of time...
she will prove you're her dream lover her fantasy...
When a woman loves it's hard...
when it's not given back...
she still picks up the slack...
When a woman loves it's till death do we part...
cause she just can't get that love out of her heart....

BY: MS: F0.XXXY

WOMAN IN THE MIRROR

MJ REMAKE

Time to make a change,

got to finnaly do whats right,

I woke up this morning to the world opening my eyes,

so much pain,

so many with nowhere to go,

children being used and abused,

a society that don't want to let go,

It's got to start from inside,

can no longer be blind,

I'm starting with the woman I see In the mirror,

I've got to change my views,

change what I see in the news,

be a voice,

for those who can't speak,

stand tall for those who are weak,

it starts with me,

how can I make a change if I don't look inside of me,

Love has never crossed my path,

been untouched,

THE FIRM DIVAS

by the one who has loved,

I need to realize,

that I'm the one with the broken heart,

got to fix me,

I can only start with the woman in the mirror,

only I can make that change,

faith doesn't come easy,

but if you wanna make a change you have to have faith,

broken,

misguided,

lied to and blinded,

but if I don't look at that woman in the mirror,

the world will never change,

need to lift myself,

and make that change!!!

BY: MS.F0XXXY

WRITING

Writing is my life...
Writing is my strength.
It heals me,when I'm hurting inside,
killing my heavy sighs.
It gets rid of the lumps in my throat
when anger and tears are bottle up.
Writing is my second love,
my world,
and my thoughts spoken out loud.
Writing is the key to my soul,
it helps unleash my expressions,
that are hidden within me.
And then when I'm done,
I'm back at mellow status,
which increases inner peace.
Writing puts a smile on my face and on my heart,
it's such a wonderful feeling..
when mind is cleansing.
Writing is you, me, us, and we...
because it's an art that every human being can use and see.
Writing is--my world..
which keeps me motivated and inspired.
Writing is what I admire,,
and it's helps me admire others!!!

BY: LAVENDER LADY

YOU ARE A DISEASE

You are a disease.
No known cure.
You're an infection.
You make my heart race and my blood boil.
Fever reaches its highest peak.
I've taken the pill,
got the injection but still no relief.
You're in the water supply.
You creep,
you crawl,
your tentacles seep in through every crack and crevice.
You grow and reach new levels at others expense.
You're a biohazars at best.
I'd put you in a barrel and bury you miles underground but somehow you'd
leak out.
Youer w weapon of mass destruction.
Known around the world and depsied by all.
Scientists rush to stop your strian,
but you change your DNA structure. Your chemical base is always
reforming,
regathering,
all-knowing.
Think I found what it takes to get rid of you.
Happiness.
Self-confidence.
Self-awareness.
The big one Love.
I remain DIVA Strong!
You're dismissed!!!

B: DARKANGEL68

YOU HAVE A LOT TO SEE

LOST WAGES
BURNING RAGES
INSTINCTS TO HOLLAR
NO CLUE OF THE NEXT DOLLAR
INNER WORTH NOT SEEN
ACCUSATIONS BLOWN TO THE EXTREME
DOING ALL YOU CAN AND STILL NOT ENOUGH
BACK IN THE RACE OF THINGS BEING ROUGH
NEVER GIVEN A WARNING, ALWAYS TOLD THINGS WERE FINE
BEING LET GO WAS HARD TO PROCESS IN MY MIND
DEMONS OF LOW ESTEEM TRYING TO CORRUPT
DID'NT KNOW ON THAT DAY THINGS WOULD BE SO ABRUPT
THE IDEA OF THEM NOT NEEDING ME ANYMORE
JUST WHEN MY INDEPENDENCE HAD STARTED TO SOAR
THEY NEVER LIKED ME FROM THE MOMENT I WALKED IN
NEVER HAD A LADY LIKE ME WITH THE COLOR OF MY SKIN
MAYBE IT'S BECAUSE I NEVER SAID YES SIR OR YES MAM
IT'S HARD TO SAY I DON'T GIVE A DAMN
INNER URGES TO WITHDRAW FROM ALL PUBLIC CONTACT
GOD RENEWING MY STRENGTH AND REASSURING HE HAS MY
BACK
I FEEL LIKE TELLING EVERYONE TO JUST LET ME BE
GOD SAID PUT ON YOUR CLOTHES BECAUSE YOU HAVE A LOT
TO SEE
EVEN IF IT'S ONLY A SMILE ON A CHILD'S FACE
GO AND FEEL THE SUN, AND BE REMINDED OF MY GRACE
THERE'S GONNA BE TEST AND TRIALS EVERYDAY
STAND STRONG AND DON'T FORGET TO PRAY
THEY NEVER LIKED JESUS WHEN HE WAS AROUND
SO START SMILING BECAUSE YOU HAVE NO REASON TO BE
DOWN

THE FIRM DIVAS

MY GRACE IS SUFFICIENT AND ENOUGH
IT'S WHAT YOU NEED WHEN TIMES ARE TOUGH
YOU STILL HAVE FOOD, A ROOF OVER YOUR HEAD, EVEN A BED
TO REST YOUR HEAD
YOU HAVE A LOT TO SEE... JUST TRUST ME... YOU HAVE A LOT
TO SEE!!!

BY: CARAMELCAKE

THE LYRICIST FIRM

ABOUT US:

thelyricistfirm@gmail.com
http://thelyricistfirm.com

WE ARE ***"THE LYRICIST FIRM LLC."*** **"TLF"**. AN "ORGANIZED FAMILY" OF WRITERS WHO HAVE COME TOGETHER TO PROMOTE "SELF AWARENESS" THROUGH A MEANS OF VARIOUS FORMS OF POETICAL LYRICS IN REHERSED/UNREHERSED... FREESTYLES, VERSES, SHORT & LONG STORIES. WE WRITE OVER MANY TOPICS OF TODAYS ISSUES, CLEAN, EXPLICED, AND SOME VERY GRAPHICAL VIEWS. POINTS OF VIEWS CAN BE HUMOROUS, SAD, HORRIFIC, SUSPENCEFUL, DRAMATIC, ROMANTIC, EDUCATIONAL, SEXUAL, RIGHTEOUS, ANGRY, JOYFUL, AND EVEN "VERY CONTREVERIAL!!!

HOWEVER:

AS IT IS, WE ARE WRITERS WITH UNHEARD VOICES DYING TO BE HEARD. FOR ***THE LYRICIST FIRM LLC.*** THIS IS MEARLY A FORM OF ENTERTAINMENT.

WE THANK YOU...

ALL OUR READERS AND SUPPORTERS FOR MAKING THIS EVENTFUL AND VERY MUCH POSSIBLE.

www.ingramcontent.com/pod-product-compliance
Lightning Source LLC
Chambersburg PA
CBHW081630040426
42449CB00014B/3246